DORSET

CITY AND COUNTY HISTORIES

General Editor: Lionel Munby
Board of Extra-Mural Studies,
University of Cambridge
Editor of *The Local Historian*

Published

TYNESIDE	C. M. Fraser and K. Emsley

In preparation

CORNWALL	Lawrence S. Snell
DERBYSHIRE	John Heath
DURHAM	B. K. Roberts
GLAMORGAN	John Davies
LANCASHIRE	J. D. Marshall
NOTTINGHAM	Alan Rogers
THE POTTERIES	Michael Greenslade and Denis Stuart
SOMERSET	R. W. Dunning
SOUTH YORKSHIRE	Derek Holland
SUFFOLK	John Ridgard
SURREY	A. R. and R. A. Michell
TEESSIDE	Barry Harrison

CITY AND COUNTY HISTORIES

DORSET

J. H. BETTEY

DAVID & CHARLES
Newton Abbot London
North Pomfret (VT) Vancouver

ISBN 0 7153 6371 9

Set in 12pt on 13pt Bembo
and printed in Great Britain
by Latimer Trend & Company Ltd Plymouth
for David & Charles (Holdings) Limited
South Devon House Newton Abbot Devon

Published in the United States of America
by David & Charles Inc
North Pomfret Vermont 05053 USA

Published in Canada
by Douglas David & Charles Limited
3645 McKechnie Drive West Vancouver BC

CONTENTS

LIST OF ILLUSTRATIONS

PREFACE

THIS book aims to give a concise introduction to the long and often complex story of the development of the county of Dorset. Within the compass of a short book it has not been possible to give detailed information on many topics, and omissions have been inevitable, but it is hoped that the short bibliography at the end of each chapter and the general bibliography at the end of the book may be of help to those who wish to pursue particular subjects. Although Dorset does not have any very imposing landward boundaries, it has a unique and very distinctive character. This is largely accounted for by the great variety of geological formations which the county contains; and perhaps much of the secret of its great charm lies in the wealth of different landscapes which this varied geology creates in such a comparatively small area. For the historian, however, this means that it is very difficult to generalise about the development of the county, for the lives, work and settlements of the people living on the heathlands of east Dorset or around the shores of Poole harbour differed widely from, for example, those of the inhabitants of the chalk downlands or of the farmers in the low-lying clay vales of the west of the county. In order to follow more closely the major lines of development in the history of the county, and to include as much detail of the life and work of the people as limited length would allow, it was decided not to adhere to a completely chronological approach, but to deal separately with some of the most important topics, while providing cross-references where needed.

There is no recent, short history of the county, but there are a number of excellent books on particular aspects of its history, and some of these are listed in the bibliographies. In addition there is a vast amount of material in the long series of the *Proceedings of the Dorset Natural History and Archaeological Society* and the *Somerset and Dorset Notes and Queries*. There is also the immensely valuable early history of the county by the Reverend John Hutchins, first published in 1774. An indispensable source for all historians is the survey of all published material which relates to the county—*A Handbook of Local History: Dorset* by Robert Douch (1962). Two aspects of the history of the county have already been dealt with in very great detail. The buildings and earthworks have been meticulously described in the volumes of the Royal Commission on Historical Monuments (England), and, more briefly but still with a tremendous amount of valuable detail, in *The Buildings of England: Dorset* by John Newman and Nikolaus Pevsner (1972). The development of the landscape of Dorset has been splendidly elucidated in *The Making of the English Landscape: Dorset* by Christopher Taylor (1970). Since these books are readily available and will already be familiar to many readers, little has been said on these subjects in the present work.

I am indebted to many friends and colleagues with whom I have discussed various aspects of Dorset history or who have helped me in other ways, in particular to Mr Robert Machin and Mr Bernard Lane. The members of numerous university extra-mural courses which I have conducted over the past few years have also made many valuable comments and suggestions. I have been greatly helped by Miss Margaret Holmes and the staff of the Dorset County Record Office, and my special thanks are due to Miss Holmes who read several of the chapters and made many helpful comments and suggestions. I have relied greatly on the resources of the County Reference Library, and on the magnificent collection of Dorset material in the Library of the Dorset Natural History and Archaeological Society. Mr Roger Peers, the Secretary of that society, who has a great knowledge of the county and of its prehistory and archaeology, kindly read and commented on some of the chapters. Mr J. H. P. Gibb has very generously allowed me to use his reconstruction of the former Saxon cathedral at Sherborne. I am grateful to Miss Maria Vincent for so cheerfully coping with the problems of turning my handwriting into typescript. Finally I would like to thank the general editor of the series, Mr Lionel Munby, who first suggested the idea of this book to me, for his encouragement and advice.

J. H. B.

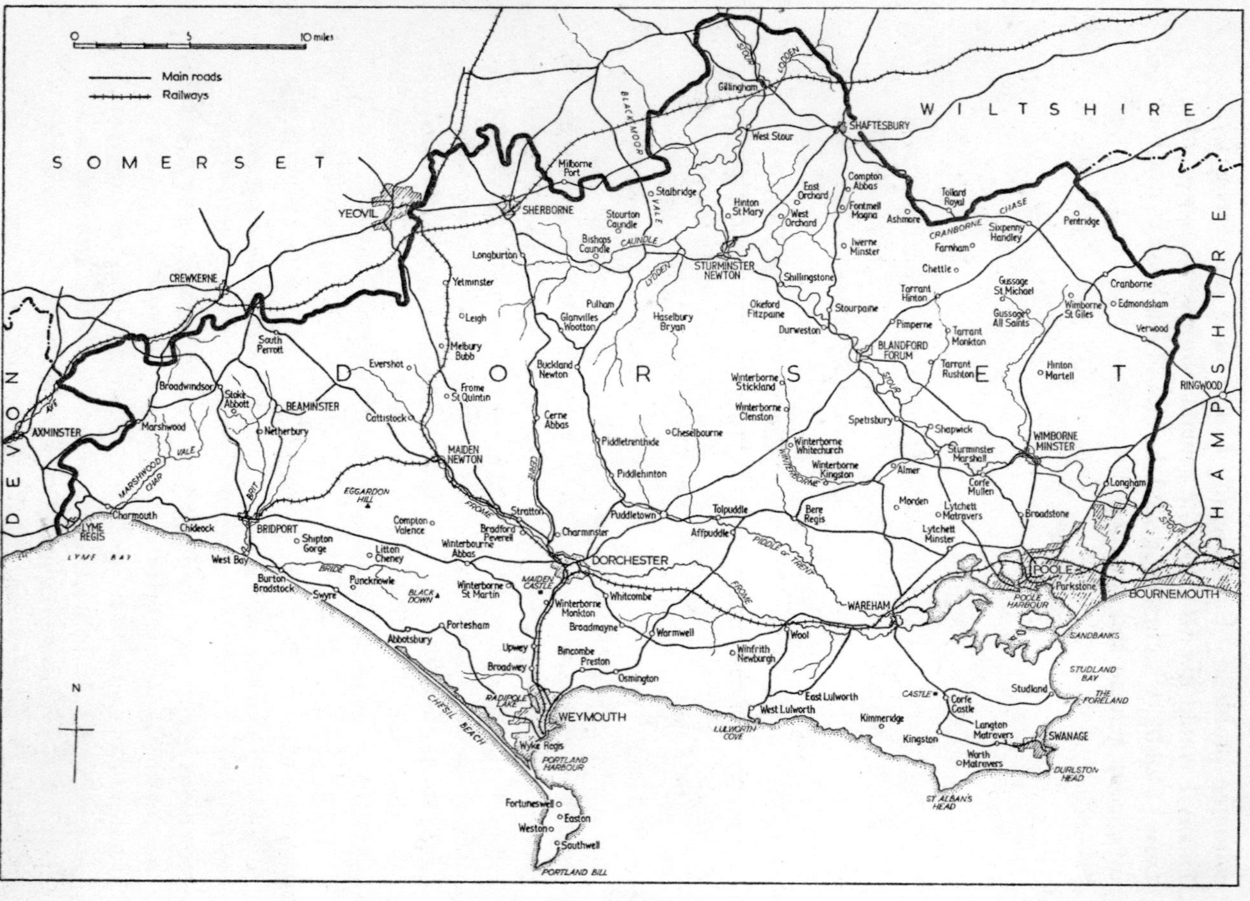
0
5
10 miles
Main roads
Railways
SOMERSET
WILTSHIRE
HAMPSHIRE
DEVON
DORSET
YEOVIL
SHERBORNE
Milborne Port
Stalbridge
Gillingham
SHAFTESBURY
West Stour
Hinton St Mary
East Orchard
West Orchard
Compton Abbas
Fontmell Magna
Iwerne Minster
Ashmore
Tollard Royal
CRANBORNE CHASE
Sixpenny Handley
Farnham
Pentridge
Cranborne
Edmondsham
Verwood
RINGWOOD
CREWKERNE
Stourton Caundle
Bishops Caundle
CAUNDLE
VALE
BLACKMOOR
STOUR
LODDEN
LYDDEN
Longburton
Yetminster
Leigh
Melbury Bubb
STURMINSTER NEWTON
Shillingstone
Stourpaine
Chettle
Tarrant Hinton
Gussage St Michael
Gussage All Saints
Wimborne St Giles
South Perrott
Pulham
Glanvilles Wootton
Haselbury Bryan
Okeford Fitzpaine
Durweston
Pimperne
Tarrant Monkton
BLANDFORD FORUM
Tarrant Rushton
Hinton Martell
Evershot
Frome St Quintin
Buckland Newton
Winterborne Stickland
Winterborne Clenston
Broadwindsor
Stoke Abbott
BEAMINSTER
Netherbury
Cattistock
AXMINSTER
AXE
Marshwood
MARSHWOOD VALE
MAIDEN NEWTON
Cerne Abbas
CERNE
Piddletrenthide
Cheselbourne
Winterborne Whitechurch
Winterborne Kingston
WINTERBORNE
Spetisbury
Shapwick
Sturminster Marshall
WIMBORNE MINSTER
Almer
Corfe Mullen
Longham
Piddlehinton
EGGARDON HILL
BRIT
Charmouth
LYME REGIS
LYME BAY
Chideock
BRIDPORT
Shipton Gorge
Compton Valence
Litton Cheney
Stratton
Bradford Peverell
Winterbourne Abbas
Charminster
Puddletown
Tolpuddle
Affpuddle
Bere Regis
Morden
Lytchett Matravers
Lytchett Minster
Broadstone
West Bay
Burton Bradstock
BRIDE
Swyre
Puncknowle
BLACK DOWN
Winterborne St Martin
MAIDEN CASTLE
DORCHESTER
FROME
PIDDLE or TRENT
POOLE
Parkstone
BOURNEMOUTH
POOLE HARBOUR
Portesham
Abbotsbury
Winterborne Monkton
Whitcombe
Broadmayne
Warmwell
Wool
WAREHAM
SANDBANKS
Upwey
Broadwey
Bincombe
Preston
Osmington
Winfrith Newburgh
STUDLAND BAY
Studland
THE FORELAND
N
CHESIL BEACH
RADIPOLE LAKE
WEYMOUTH
East Lulworth
West Lulworth
LULWORTH COVE
CASTLE
Corfe Castle
Kimmeridge
Kingston
Langton Matravers
SWANAGE
Worth Matravers
DURLSTON HEAD
ST ALBAN'S HEAD
Wyke Regis
PORTLAND HARBOUR
Fortuneswell
Easton
Weston
Southwell
PORTLAND BILL

Fig 1 Dorset

Chapter 1 PREHISTORIC AND ROMAN DORSET

THE earliest evidence of human habitation in the area which was later to be known as Dorset comes from the Palaeolithic or Old Stone Age. During this period of comparative warmth between the Ice Ages, traces of human occupation in the form of flint tools have been found at various places, including Moreton on the river Frome and Corfe Mullen on the Stour, and at Sherborne. The very scattered occupation of the area which the finds suggest, was ended by the last glacial period. After about 10,000 BC the climate slowly improved thus creating conditions in which a sparse population of Mesolithic hunters could survive. Some 150 sites of Mesolithic occupation have been found in Dorset, including important settlements at Portland, along the north shore of the Fleet, in the Stour valley and in the area of Corfe Mullen, overlooking Poole harbour. These people lived by hunting, fishing and collecting wild fruit, seeds, shell-fish etc, and probably did not stay for long in any one place, but travelled widely over southern England in search of food.

From about 3500 BC onwards the scattered Mesolithic people were joined by immigrants from the Continent who have left a much more clearly marked archaeological record of their settlement in the area. These were the Neolithic settlers, a much more advanced group, who kept domestic animals, used pottery, and grew crops of wheat and barley. Their agriculture was probably semi-nomadic, and little is known of their settlements, though sites at Corfe Mullen and near Wimborne have been partially excavated. The most important and characteristic sites associated with the Neolithic people are the causewayed enclosures and the long barrows. The former are circular or oval enclosures with one or more banks and ditches, and with gaps or causeways in the banks. The purpose of these sites is obscure, though it seems clear that they were not lived in, and were perhaps used as meeting places or possibly for herding cattle. Two such causewayed enclosures have been found at Maiden Castle and at Hambledon Hill where they lie beneath or beside the much later Iron Age hillforts. The long barrows or burial mounds of the Neolithic period are much more conspicuous in Dorset, since some forty of them are known, and some, such as those at Pimperne and Long Bredy, are particularly fine and well preserved. The Neolithic people were also responsible for the strange earthwork known as the Dorset 'Cursus' on Cranborne Chase, which consists of two parallel banks running for six and a half miles across country from Thickthorn Down north-east across the Chase almost to Bokerley Dyke. This is one of the great monuments of prehistoric Britain, but there is little agreement as to its purpose. Three other ritual sites or 'henge' monuments also date from this period. These are Maumbury Rings, the impressive earthwork on the outskirts of Dorchester, Mount Pleasant, on the other side of Dorchester, and Knowlton, on the road between Cranborne and Wimborne, where the ruins of Knowlton Church now occupy the area inside the rampart. It is certain that people who could undertake the building of such monuments had an extraordinary degree of organisation and a way of life which allowed considerable leisure from the elementary business of obtaining food and shelter.

THE BRONZE AGE

Around 2000 BC another group of settlers arrived, the first of the Bronze Age peoples, known as the 'Beaker People' from the type of pottery vessel associated with them. Technically more advanced than existing inhabitants, their farming was very similar, and they grew wheat and barley and kept domestic animals, including sheep from whose wool they wove cloth. The most obvious remaining evidences of their presence in Dorset are the round barrows in which they buried their dead. Many hundreds of these survive and a great many more have been destroyed. Often the barrows are strung out along the skyline, and were obviously very carefully sited to be visible from the valleys, where perhaps the relatives of the deceased lived.

Many examples of this are to be seen, for example, on Oakley Down, near Wimborne St Giles, and in the area around Dorchester. The South Dorset Ridgeway has the greatest number of barrows in any area of the country, and the largest group of all is at Poor Lot, near Winterbourne Abbas where there are no less than forty-four barrows. Many of these barrows have been greatly damaged during the past few years by modern ploughing, and Mr Roger Peers has recently drawn attention to the disturbing fact that less than 15 per cent of the barrows in the county now remain unharmed.

Other settlers followed the earliest Bronze Age people, and there appear to have been a series of migrations into Dorset in the centuries around 1000 BC. But relatively little is known of this period and only one site in Dorset has been excavated, at Sydling St Nicholas on the chalk downland north of Dorchester. This was a farm surrounded by the typical small, rectangular and square fields of the period. Evidence from this excavation and from elsewhere in the county suggests that the people living in Dorset at this time were practising a mixed farming economy, and that they had already achieved a relatively high standard with considerable trade in their characteristic bronze implements and objects. Christopher Taylor in his recent work on the landscape of Dorset has argued very convincingly and interestingly that the settlements of this period were not confined to the high ground, but occupied a good deal of lower lying land in the sheltered valleys of the chalklands where lighter soils made this practicable. Later settlement and agriculture have however destroyed almost all evidence except on the higher ground. The sites on higher ground may indeed be some evidence that there was already pressure of population in the more sheltered areas which forced some people to live in the more exposed places.

Certainly population increased considerably in the Iron Age, from about 550 BC, when Dorset became the centre of the Durotriges, a tribe whose territory included Dorset and the fringes of the surrounding counties. The best known and most characteristic Iron Age sites are the great hilltop fortresses. Dorset is particularly rich in splendid examples of these massive fortifications ranging from the great complex of multiple earthworks at Maiden Castle (occupying some forty-seven acres) or the great forts at Hambledon, Hod Hill, Badbury Rings or Eggardon, to the small sites of Rawlsbury on Bulbarrow Hill or Crawford Castle at Spetisbury. There are twenty-seven such sites in Dorset and the tremendous effort and labour involved in their construction, shows that the society was already highly organised and suggests also that there was a very real need for protection from hostile forces. Their number and distribution also provides evidence of a very considerable population occupying and cultivating both high and low lying land in most parts of the county. The fields or arable plots of these Iron Age farmers are still clearly to be seen over wide areas of the chalk downlands of Dorset. By the first century BC, the Durotriges had achieved a sophisticated way of life, with a developed agricultural and pastoral farming economy, a system of currency using metal coins, and specialised industries such as pottery, salt extraction along the coast, and the quarrying of Kimmeridge shale for ornaments, as well as trade across the channel.

THE ROMAN CONQUEST

The conquest of the south-west of England was undertaken by the Roman forces very soon after their landing at Richborough in the late summer of AD 43. The task of subduing the Durotriges of Dorset, strongly entrenched behind their massive hillforts, was given by the Roman commander Aulus Plautius to his most trusted lieutenant, Vespasian (later Emperor), who led the II Augusta Legion. The historical evidence of the campaign rests on the few details given in the biography of Vespasian by Suetonius. This states that in Britain, Vespasian 'fought thirty battles, subjugated two warlike tribes and captured more than twenty

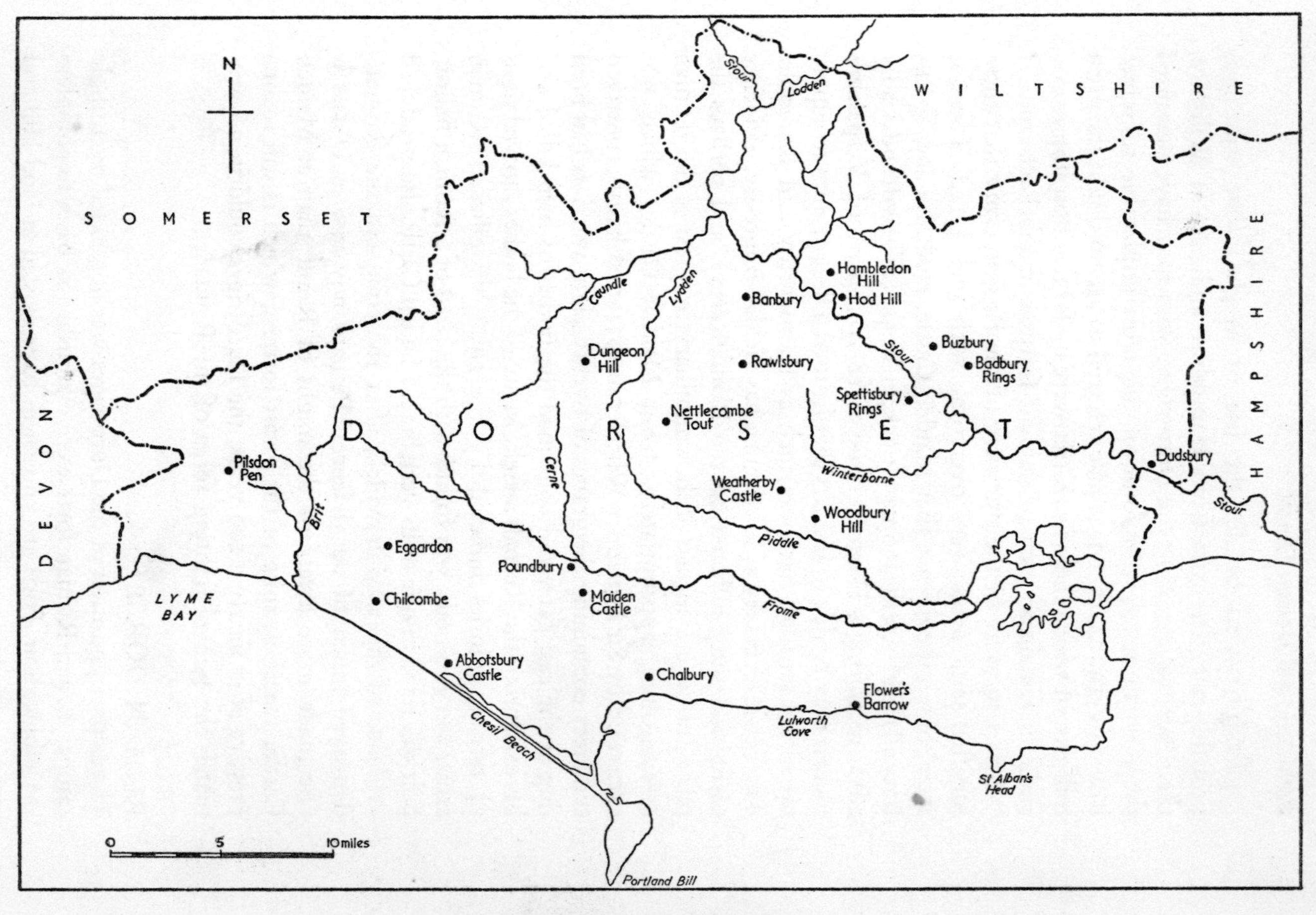

Fig 2 Major Iron Age hillforts

oppida (fortresses) besides the Isle of Wight'. One tribe was probably the Atrebates from Hampshire and part of Wiltshire, the other was certainly the Durotriges, who may have presented the Roman army with some of the most implacable resistance it was to encounter. The *oppida* referred to are no doubt the great hillforts, of which those in Dorset were by far the most impressive, and still remain as such prominent features of the landscape.

It is a measure of the efficiency of the Roman army that these fortified settlements were overcome with such speed. There is archaeological evidence that Maiden Castle, Hod Hill and Spetisbury all fell before the Roman attack, in Vespasian's swift and deadly advance through Dorset to the river Axe. Part of Vespasian's success may be due to the fact that he used a fleet of ships to supply his forces through harbours such as Hamworthy and Radipole. The battle cemetery at Spetisbury has yielded impressive evidence of the slaughter inflicted by the Roman army, and perhaps the most dramatic evidence of the sanguinary progress of the Roman army comes, appropriately, from Maiden Castle, which was excavated by Sir Mortimer Wheeler in 1934–7. A hastily contrived cemetery containing the graves of twenty-eight warriors had been dug at the east gate, and contained the bodies of men killed and buried during the Roman attack. Many of the bodies showed signs of terrible injuries inflicted by the ruthlessly efficient Roman arms, and one body was found with the head of a Roman ballista bolt still fixed in one of its vertebrae. Maiden Castle also produced evidence of the way in which, after the conquest, the Romans destroyed much of the defences. Perhaps nowhere in Dorset is one made more aware of the might of Rome than at Maiden Castle, where in spite of their vast fortress, which is still so impressive after nearly 2,000 years, the Durotriges could in no way match the trained fighting force of the Romans.

ROMAN DORSET

The fierce opposition of the Durotriges was not ended by a single campaign, and Roman forts were established as bases to complete the subjugation. Forts are known to have existed at Hod Hill and

Waddon Hill and there were certainly more, but the chief sign of Roman domination must have been the great roads. Moreover the employment of great numbers of native labourers upon their construction must have given many their first intimate taste of Roman rule.

By far the most important town to be founded was Durnovaria, later Dorchester, which was founded about AD 70 on the road from London to Exeter via Silchester, Old Sarum and Badbury (Vindocladia). The site was defended at first by earthen ramparts, traces of which are still to be seen, and later by stone walls. Most of the Roman town has been destroyed by later building, but the notable Roman town house with its foundations complete can be seen in Colliton Park, by the modern County Hall. Durnovaria was particularly notable for its water supply, brought by a remarkable aqueduct from several miles away, and for its great amphitheatre, the adapted henge monument at Maumbury Rings just outside the town which is still so impressive. The later streets of Dorchester have destroyed most of the Roman town, but enough survives in the area and in the County Museum to provide a powerful reminder of the former importance of Durnovaria.

During the centuries of Roman peace, population in Dorset increased considerably, and new land was brought into cultivation, particularly on the chalk downlands. By the second century of Roman rule, villas were being established in many places in the area. Known sites are most numerous in the valleys, particularly along the Frome and in the Blackmoor Vale, but it is probable that many sites are located beneath modern villages and remain unrecognised. Villas with mosaics showing very considerable sophistication have been found in several parts of the county, and three of them show evidence of Christianity—those from Frampton, Fifehead Neville and the most outstanding of all, with a human figure almost certainly a representation of Christ, from Hinton St Mary. In addition there was a large Roman temple built inside Maiden Castle, and another at Jordon Hill near Weymouth.

It is possible that it was during the period of Roman occupation that the remarkable figure of the Cerne Giant was cut. He certainly resembles Roman representations of Hercules. But remarkably little is known with certainty concerning this strange, pagan and aggressively masculine figure which still dominates Cerne Abbas, and which once must incongruously have overshadowed the Benedictine Abbey there. Curiously, no documentary reference to his existence is to be found until the eighteenth century, though considerable labour must have been involved in scouring the outline of the figure every few years, and Cerne is particularly rich in documentary sources of information on other aspects of its history.

SELECT BIBLIOGRAPHY

Royal Commission on Historical Monuments (England), volumes on Dorset (hereafter R.C.H.M. *Dorset*)

Many important articles and reports of excavations are included in the *Proceedings of the Dorset Natural History and Archaeological Society* (hereafter *Dorset Proceedings*)

The best authoritative summary of the present state of archaeological knowledge is in the section by Roger Peers on 'Prehistoric and Roman Remains' in J. Newman and N. Pevsner, *The Buildings of England—Dorset* (1972)

O. G. S. Crawford and A. Keiller — *Wessex from the Air* (1928)

P. J. Fowler — *Wessex* (1967)

L. V. Grinsell — *The Archaeology of Wessex* (1958); *Dorset Barrows* (1959)

N. H. Field and J. Bugler — *The Guide to the Field Monuments of Dorset* (1973)

Chapter 2 THE ENGLISH CONQUEST AND SETTLEMENT AND THE NORMAN CONQUEST

THE chronology of the Saxon conquest of Dorset presents very considerable difficulties, since the evidence is sparse and complicated. It is clear that after the Roman army was finally recalled early in the fifth century, there was a period of more than two hundred years before the Saxon invasion made any serious impact on Dorset. During this long period, Romano-British life continued with apparently little break. No doubt the withdrawal of the Roman army and administration had important effects, and there is evidence of decline in living standards during the period. But the change was probably felt most in Dorchester and in the villas, while in the great number of Romano-British settlements and farms the way of life continued very much as in the period of Roman occupation. Meanwhile the Saxon invaders had conquered and settled very extensively in the surrounding region. By the middle of the sixth century they had advanced from the Southampton-Portsmouth area, through Hampshire, had defeated the Britons at the Iron Age fort of Old Sarum, and had continued across Wiltshire. The *Anglo-Saxon Chronicle* gives the date of this battle as 552, and goes on to mention a battle at Dyrham, north of Bath, in 577 which gave the Saxons control of that area.

Early in the seventh century the Saxon invaders were penetrating deeply into Somerset. One reason why Dorset was able to hold out against the invaders so much longer than the neighbouring areas may have been that, as at the time of the Roman conquest, the quality of the resistance which the Britons in Dorset put up was very high. The prosperity of Dorset built up during the Roman period no doubt provided a very considerable motive for fierce resistance to the invaders, and the most spectacular evidence of this is to be found in the great defensive earthwork of Bokerley Dyke. This enormous defence, stretching for some six miles across the neck of downland in the north-east of the county, blocks the main approach into the county from the north. It dates originally from the late fourth century, but after the departure of the Romans it was repaired, and when manned by Britons intent on preserving their homelands it undoubtedly presented a formidable obstacle to the invading Saxons. It still forms the county boundary. Recent work on this period has also provided a further fascinating piece of evidence concerning the resistance put up by the Britons of Dorset. A number of independent literary sources concerning the Saxon invasions mention a great British victory over the invaders in about the year 500 at a place called Mons Badonicus, or Mount Badon. The battle is mentioned by the monk Gildas, writing about 545, as a tremendous victory for the Britons (perhaps under Arthur, though Gildas, the earliest source, does not mention him. He does claim that the Saxons were so crushed at the battle that for a long time they did not take up arms again). Many suggestions have been put forward concerning the site of Mount Badon, but recent work has very plausibly identified it with Badbury Rings. If this is accepted, it is further striking evidence of the difficulty which the Saxons, like the Romans before them, encountered in conquering the Durotrigian region, and provides part of the answer to the puzzling question of why Dorset remained so long free from Saxon invasion. The fact that the Saxon conquest of Dorset was so long delayed is striking proof of the numbers, strength and organisation of the post-Roman society in the area, and of the economic prosperity which enabled the defences to be maintained.

Dorset could not hold out for ever against the Saxons, particularly after they had established themselves in the neighbouring areas. There is some evidence of Saxon invasion of Dorset by sea, but this is sparse, partly because only a few of the likely archaeological sites have as yet been properly investigated, though Saxon burials have been found near Charmouth, at the mouth of the river Stour and on Cranborne Chase. The main, and final, Saxon attack came after 665, when the Saxons broke through the British defences. The defensive earthwork of Bokerley Dyke was pierced, and although a second line of defence at Combs Ditch some fifteen miles inside the county boundary was manned for a time, this did not hold back the invaders for long, and in the decade following 665 they had reached Dorchester and the rest of the county was rapidly overrun.

It is likely, however, that the British people of Dorset were left relatively undisturbed by the small warrior class of Saxons who had conquered them. It is true that the evidence of the Dorset place names would indicate a fairly substantial Saxon settlement since the majority of the names are Saxon. But too much importance cannot be attached to this for it is clear that bilingualism long persisted in Dorset. At Wareham a number of Celtic inscriptions in the Church of Lady St Mary show the survival of a reasonably well-off British population at least into the eighth century, and the river names of Dorset remain Celtic. It is probable that the impact of the Saxon conquest upon the Britons of Dorset was not great. The Saxons were relatively few in number, a warrior aristocracy, and, apart from bringing Dorset into the main stream of Wessex religious and cultural life, they did not drive out or exterminate the existing inhabitants.

One result of the late conquest of Dorset by the Saxons was that by the time it took place the Saxons were already Christian, and missionaries rapidly followed the conquerors. There is little evidence to indicate how much of the Christianity which had existed in Dorset during the Roman period survived the withdrawal of the Roman armies, though the unique series of inscriptions in the church of Lady St Mary at Wareham, which range in date from the seventh to the ninth century, suggest that some Christian worship may have continued. At all events, Christianity spread rapidly after the Saxon conquest and a great step forward in the formal organisation of the church in Dorset came in the reign of Ine, king of Wessex (688–725), by the creation of the see of Sherborne with Aldhelm, friend and kinsman of Ine, as its first bishop. The new diocese comprised much of the recent additions to the kingdom of Wessex and included the whole of Dorset and Somerset, and probably also Devon and Cornwall. Aldhelm was consecrated as first bishop of Sherborne in 705.

Aldhelm is the first person of note connected with Dorset of whose life and personality we know anything more than the barest outline, and of whose personality we can form some opinion. This is due largely to the *Life* written by William of Malmesbury, the great English historian of the twelfth century, who, like Aldhelm, was a Benedictine monk at Malmesbury. Aldhelm was born about 639, and his father, Centen, was a near relative of Ine, later to be king of Wessex. As a member of the royal family, he received a careful and lengthy education first at Malmesbury, where he was taught by an Irish hermit named Maeldub, and later, as a young man, at the school at Canterbury. From Canterbury his reputation as a scholar became known, even on the Continent, and Aldhelm began the series of letters, verses and discourses which make him the outstanding scholar of the period. But Aldhelm was not only a great scholar of the seventh century in England, he was also a man of very deep piety, and capable of arousing great love and devotion in others. An accomplished musician and minstrel, and a captivating preacher, Aldhelm lives for us in a way that few other figures of the pre-Norman Conquest period do.

In about 675 Aldhelm was ordained priest and returned from Canterbury to Malmesbury as first abbot of the newly founded monastery there. His work at Malmesbury lies outside the scope of this study, but Aldhelm remained at Malmesbury until 705 where he achieved great success founding other monasteries at Frome and Bradford on Avon, and becoming very widely known for his piety and scholarship. Whilst he was abbot of Malmesbury, Aldhelm paid his first visit to Dorset on the first stage of a journey to Rome. He took ship from Wareham, already an important town and sea-port. William of Malmesbury records that whilst waiting for favourable winds at Wareham, Aldhelm built a church in the area.

In 705 Aldhelm was consecrated as the first bishop of the new diocese of Sherborne, and ruled over it until his death in 709. Unfortunately we know far less of his episcopate than we do of his time at Malmesbury. William of Malmesbury tells us that, as bishop of Sherborne, 'He constantly preached by night and day, diligently travelled throughout his diocese, and was faithful in fasting and good works as in his prime.' At Sherborne he commenced the building of a great cathedral church on the site of the present abbey church, with a house for the clergy to the west of the church, probably occupying the site of the present vicarage. He died in the spring of 709 at Doulting in Somerset whilst he was visiting that part of his diocese, and was buried at Malmesbury.

An even earlier religious foundation was already established in Dorset when Aldhelm became bishop of Sherborne in 705. This was the nunnery at Wimborne founded by two sisters of King Ine, Cuthburga and Coenburga, who successively ruled over it. The foundation at Wimborne was a so-called 'double monastery', that is, it consisted of two quite separate establishments—one for men, the other for women. The monastery at Wimborne gained prominence in the ninth century though its association with St Boniface, the missionary to Germany, who came originally from Crediton in Devon. Several nuns from Wimborne followed him to Germany, among them Lioba who became one of his foremost assistants. Her biography written by a monk in Germany during the ninth century gives a detailed account of the organisation and life of the monastery at Wimborne. Another nunnery existed at Wareham, though this was destroyed by the Vikings in 878 and little is known about it.

The organisation of the Church in Dorset into the now-familiar pattern of parishes, each with its church, did not of course take place immediately after the spread of Christianity. This arrangement emerged slowly and was not complete at the time of the

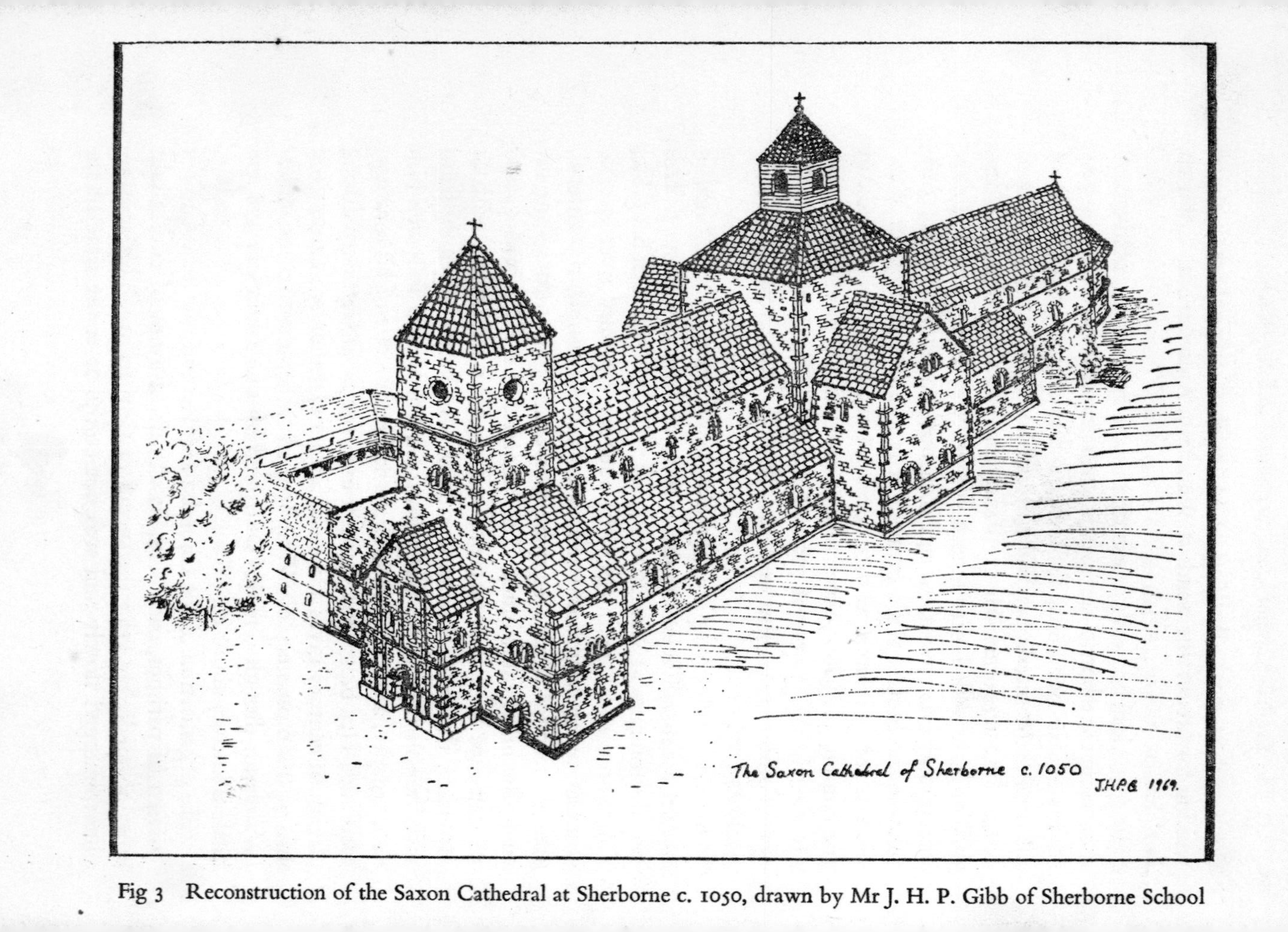

Fig 3 Reconstruction of the Saxon Cathedral at Sherborne c. 1050, drawn by Mr J. H. P. Gibb of Sherborne School

Domesday Survey in 1086. The first stage in the process in England, as on the Continent, was the establishment of 'minster' churches, some of which were monasteries while others were staffed by secular clergy living in a community. From these centres the clergy went out to preach and minister to the surrounding areas. The sites in each district at which the clergy preached and conducted the services were often marked by standing crosses, some of which remain today, though not always easily recognisable, as for example the superbly carved cross shaft at Melbury Bubb which has been converted into a font or the upper part of a tenth-century cross shaft in the church at Yetminster. In time most of the crosses were replaced by churches, and many of the minster churches in Dorset can be identified either by the fact that the word 'minster' is still combined in the name as at Beaminster, Yetminster, Sturminster, etc, or by the known antiquity and importance of the church as at Sherborne or Wareham. Sometimes a clue may be obtained from a Saxon dedication as at Whitchurch Canonicorum, which has the typically Saxon double dedication to St Candida and the Holy Rood.

The Saxon conquest of Dorset in the seventh century, and Dorset's inclusion in the kingdom of Wessex, brought a century of peace in its train. This period came to an end in the ninth century with the Viking raids. The first appearance of the Vikings anywhere in southern England came in about 790 when a small party landed at Portland. The raiders came in three ships and were probably Norwegians from Horthaland. The inhabitants of Dorset were clearly quite unprepared for attacks, for the royal 'reeve', or official, Beadaheard, hearing of their arrival rode out from Dorchester with a small number of men to meet the strangers, presuming them to be traders. He was made aware of his mistake, however, when the Vikings set upon him and killed him and his companions. The raiders then left Dorset and there is no further record of any attack for more than thirty years.

The really important Viking attacks along the English Channel coast began in 835, and in the next few years there were many raids on Dorset. It was extremely difficult to organise any effective defence against such mobile attackers, though Bishop Ealhstan of Sherborne did achieve some success in defending his diocese against the heathen attacks. He died in 867 and was buried at Sherborne, having been bishop there for fifty years. But in spite of occasional successes in repelling the invaders, the raids continued unabated. In 871 Ethelred, king of Wessex, died and was buried at Wimborne—an indication of the continuing importance of the monastery there. He was succeeded by his brother, Alfred. The attacks of the Danes continued, and Alfred was forced to buy peace from the enemy. Alfred was able to use the breathing space he had purchased to build up some of the defences of his battle-worn kingdom, but in 875 the Danish army returned, under the command of Guthrum, one of the great Danish leaders, and this time their attack was made on Dorset. The Danish army occupied Wareham and devastated the surrounding area, probably as part of an elaborate plan for an attack on the Poole harbour area by the army assisted by a sea-borne force. Wareham, situated between the two rivers Frome and Piddle and therefore easily defended, was an admirable situation for a base from which to attack and conquer the rest of Dorset and extend Danish rule over this part of England. The monastery at Wareham was destroyed at this time. But fortunately for Wessex, a storm destroyed a large number of the Viking ships off Swanage. Without reinforcements, and pressed by the Wessex army under Alfred, Guthrum was forced to seek terms. In return for a money payment the Danes agreed under solemn oaths to leave Wessex, and gave hostages in guarantee of their pledge. But Guthrum did not keep his word. Under cover of darkness the Danish army slipped out of Wareham and rushed to Exeter where they established themselves before Alfred's army could overtake them. The Wessex army continued to harry them, however, and in 877 the Danes withdrew from Wessex into Mercia. Shortly after Christmas 878 they returned and occupied Chippenham, but this time Alfred was able to attack them on equal terms at Edington, and won the decisive battle of the war. He was thus able to compel Guthrum and his army finally to leave Wessex.

This ended the Danish raids, certainly as far as Dorset was concerned, and Alfred was able to consolidate his rule in Wessex, and build up its defensive system. The defence of southern England against the Danes had proved virtually impossible partly because of the lack of an adequate English naval force, and partly because of the absence of fortifications and strongholds within which the inhabitants of each area could take refuge and from which counter-attacks could be organised. By the end of Alfred's reign such centres had been established through Wessex. In Dorset, fortifications were provided at Bridport, Shaftesbury and Wareham, where extensive remains of the defences survive. Dorchester was already secure behind its Roman walls, and these four towns rapidly became the principal centres in Dorset. Striking evidence of this is provided by the fact that mints were established at all four places, a clear sign of expanding trade and commerce which grew in the new peace-time conditions.

The period of peace following the reign of Alfred also saw the foundation in Dorset of a remarkable number of important monasteries, which were to be such a notable feature of the county throughout the Middle Ages. The repeated Danish raids and invasions of the ninth century had meant that religious life in England was at a very low ebb, and monastic houses had virtually ceased to exist. In Dorset, the monastery at Wimborne had certainly declined dramatically from the great days of its association with the mission of St Boniface, and although some religious establishment may have continued to exist there, it was probably not a monastery according to the strict sense of the term. But apart from this, only the secular clergy operating from the minster churches managed to survive the Danish attacks, and although little is known of the ordinary clergy during this period, the standard of their learning and practice seems not to have been very high. Alfred's remark of 871 that he could not call to mind a single man south of the Thames who was able to follow the Mass in Latin or who could translate a letter from Latin into English, may have been exaggerated but gives some indication of contemporary clerical education. And Alfred's biographer Bishop

Asser tells us that when the king wished to re-establish monasticism he was forced to seek monks from abroad for his monasteries.

One important religious house founded by Alfred was the nunnery of Shaftesbury. This was established about the year 888 and the king appointed his daughter Ethelgifu as the first abbess of the community. Asser records that the nunnery was by the east gate of Shaftesbury and that many noble nuns joined the community, which Alfred had richly endowed with 'estates and wealth of all kinds'. These endowments were greatly increased by Alfred's successors during the tenth century, so that this community of nuns living according to the Rule of St Benedict became very wealthy.

Alfred's lead in church reform and revival was followed by his son Edward the Elder who on the death of Bishop Asser of Sherborne in 909, reorganised the dioceses of Wessex, so that the Sherborne diocese was divided. The diocese of Crediton was created to comprise Devon and Cornwall, Somerset was given its own diocese with the bishopric of Wells, while the new diocese of Sherborne consisted only of Dorset.

The Benedictine monastery at Milton was founded in 933 by King Athelstan, and, again, was very richly endowed. Other Dorset monasteries were founded during the tenth century as part of the monastic revival associated with the name of St Dunstan. From c. 940 Dunstan became abbot of Glastonbury and began the task of reviving the Benedictine monastic life at this, the most famous of English monasteries. His influence and the effect of his revived monasticism soon spread in Wessex, and had the effect of greatly stimulating the foundation of monasteries. In c. 987 a Benedictine monastery was founded at Cerne by Aethelmaer a Wessex 'thane', or nobleman. There may already have been a small group of clergy living a corporate life there, but the new foundation was established on strict Benedictine lines, and with endowments of land in various parts of Dorset. The monastery rapidly became famous for having amongst its monks the most considerable scholar and writer in the English church of the later part of the tenth century. This was Aelfric who was a monk at the Old Minster at Winchester until he was sent by Bishop Aelfheah of Winchester to instruct the monks at the new foundation at Cerne. Aelfric is second in importance only to Bede as a theologian, writer and teacher in the pre-Conquest church, and is one of the most distinguished figures in the whole history of the English Church. Much of his work was done in the seclusion and quiet of the monastery at Cerne, and Aelfric himself in the preface to the first of a constant stream of religious and devotional as well as grammatical writings and translations, says: 'I Aelfric, monk and mass-priest . . . was sent, in bishop Aethelred's day by bishop Aelfheah, Aethelred's successor, to a minster which is called Cernel at the prayer of Aethelmaer the thane.' Aelfric remained at Cerne until 1005, when he became the first abbot of the new monastery at Eynsham, near Oxford. Other religious houses were founded in Dorset during the tenth century at Cranborne and at Sherborne where in 993 the then bishop, Wulfsige, who had himself been a monk at Glastonbury under St Dunstan, made the church of Sherborne into a monastery.

The death of King Edgar, in 975, was followed by civil strife in which Dorset figured prominently. Edgar had been married twice, and left two sons. By his first wife he had a son named Edward, and by his second wife, a son named Ethelred who in 975 was no more than ten years old. Edgar's death before either of his sons reached manhood created great confusion and faction in his kingdom. Edward was crowned king, but many nobles supported Ethelred. The result of the ensuing conflict and disorder was that the slow growth of civilisation which had been taking place during the tenth century, and which is shown most clearly in the endowment of monasteries, was brought to an abrupt end.

On the surface the relationship between Edward and his half-brother Ethelred continued to be one of friendship during the years of civil dissension following their father's death, and in March 978 Edward paid an informal visit to his half-brother and his stepmother Elfthryth at Corfe. He was greeted with apparent respect and friendship, but having arrived, he was surrounded by his half-brother's retainers and supporters and brutally murdered. This dastardly crime shocked even the men of that time who were not unused to violence. The *Anglo-Saxon Chronicle* contains the dramatic entry: 'In this year King Edward was killed at the gap of Corfe on 18th March in the evening, and he was buried at Wareham without any royal honours. And no worse deed than this for the English people was committed since they first came to Britain.' The young murdered king rapidly acquired the reputation of a saint, and is remembered in history as Edward the Martyr. A year after his death, in 979, his body was moved to the house of nuns at Shaftesbury, and the shrine soon became a place of pilgrimage. As the *Anglo-Saxon Chronicle* expressed it, 'Men murdered him but God honoured him. In life he was an earthly king; he is now after death an heavenly saint.' Meanwhile Ethelred was crowned king in an atmosphere of suspicion and mistrust, which was to continue throughout his reign. Whilst the king himself was too young to be blamed for his brother's murder at Corfe, he was never able to live down the events through which he came to the throne, and his reign was plagued by violence, incapacity and vacillation.

It is no coincidence that within two years of his accession Danish raiding parties were once again landing on English shores and the second wave of invasions had begun. In 982 three Viking ships arrived off the coast of Dorset and attacked Portland. There was some respite in Dorset for a few years thereafter, but in 997 a large Danish army descended upon England, prepared to spend several years in systematic plundering. The army reached Dorset in 998, and again, the *Anglo-Saxon Chronicle* gives a dramatic description of the events: 'In this year (998) the army turned back east into the mouth of the Frome, and there they went inland everywhere into Dorset as widely as they pleased; and the English army was often assembled against them . . . and always the enemy had the victory in the end.' This miserable period of English helplessness before the Danish attacks continued for twenty years with ever more desperate expedients of Danegeld taxes to buy off the ravaging armies, until finally in 1017 Cnut, or Canute, was recognised as king of all England. Cnut himself landed in southern

England in 1015 and chose Poole harbour as his earliest base. From here his armies ravaged far and wide in Dorset and the neighbouring counties, before moving to besiege London. It is probable that the great Saxon monastery at Wimborne, so important a century earlier, was destroyed by the Danes. It was later to be refounded as a community of canons. The abbey of Cerne was also plundered, probably by raiders under Cnut himself. We know even less of the sufferings of ordinary people in Dorset, but there is no doubt that they suffered severely, plagued on the one hand by the Danish raids and the ever present threat of violence and sudden death, and on the other by lack of government and by onerous demands for taxes to pay the increasingly burdensome Danegeld.

In 1016–17 Dorset passed with the rest of Wessex into Danish rule under Cnut. Cnut, once in power in England, became a pious Christian and he and his chief magnates were the patrons of a number of monasteries. In Dorset two of his followers founded monasteries on lands granted to them by Cnut. Urk or Orc founded the monastery at Abbotsbury, while another important magnate, Bovi, founded the religious house at Horton. Thus by the time of the Norman Conquest, Dorset had no fewer than eight important religious houses.

THE NORMAN CONQUEST

Dorset suffered considerably in the upheaval following the Norman Conquest in 1066. In the first months after William's victory at Hastings, Dorset, in common with much of the South West, seems to have held out against the Normans. In January and February 1068 the men of Dorset supported Exeter in refusing to recognise William as king. William therefore led the Norman army to the South West to besiege Exeter. His course would naturally have led him through Dorset, and it was no doubt at this time that the damage and destruction which is so dramatically recorded in the Domesday Book, was wrought in the county. In particular the four Dorset boroughs of Dorchester, Bridport, Wareham and Shaftesbury were badly damaged, no doubt as part of a policy designed to intimidate Exeter.

Apart from the physical damage caused in the fighting, the chief effect of the Conquest was of course social and economic, the tenurial revolution which involved the replacement of the English landowning class by Normans. Understandably, this change did not occur without fierce opposition from the English, and in 1069 for example we hear of a joint attack by men of Dorset and Somerset on the castle being built at Montacute. This English revolt was crushed with considerable severity by an army under the great Norman warrior-bishop, Geoffrey, bishop of Coutances.

For the historian, one of the most interesting effects of the Conquest was the compilation of the Domesday Book in 1086. This gives us the first opportunity of looking in detail at the economic life of Dorset and of reconstructing its settlement pattern, and, since the Survey includes a backward look to the time when King Edward the Confessor was on the throne, it is also an authority for the extent and spread of settlement in Dorset on the eve of the Norman Conquest. The Domesday Book is not an easy record to use, and its interpretation presents many difficulties. The Survey was based on manors, and does not always mention outlying settlements and isolated farms or hamlets. Some very large manors in Dorset such as Sherborne, Portland, and Puddletown included a number of villages, whose names are not therefore recorded. Also a very large number of places in Dorset take their names from the streams along which they are situated, and it is not always easy to distinguish between several different places with the same basic name. Nonetheless it gives a remarkable amount of detailed information and is an unparalleled source for medieval local history.

The total number of separate places mentioned in the Domesday Book for the area of the modern county of Dorset is approximately 319, and these settlements were divided into thirty-nine Hundreds. Not by any means all of the places mentioned have prospered to the extent of being modern parishes, and 120 of the places mentioned are today no more than hamlets or single farms. There were four boroughs in the county whose names appear at the beginning of the Dorset section—Dorchester, Bridport, Shaftesbury and

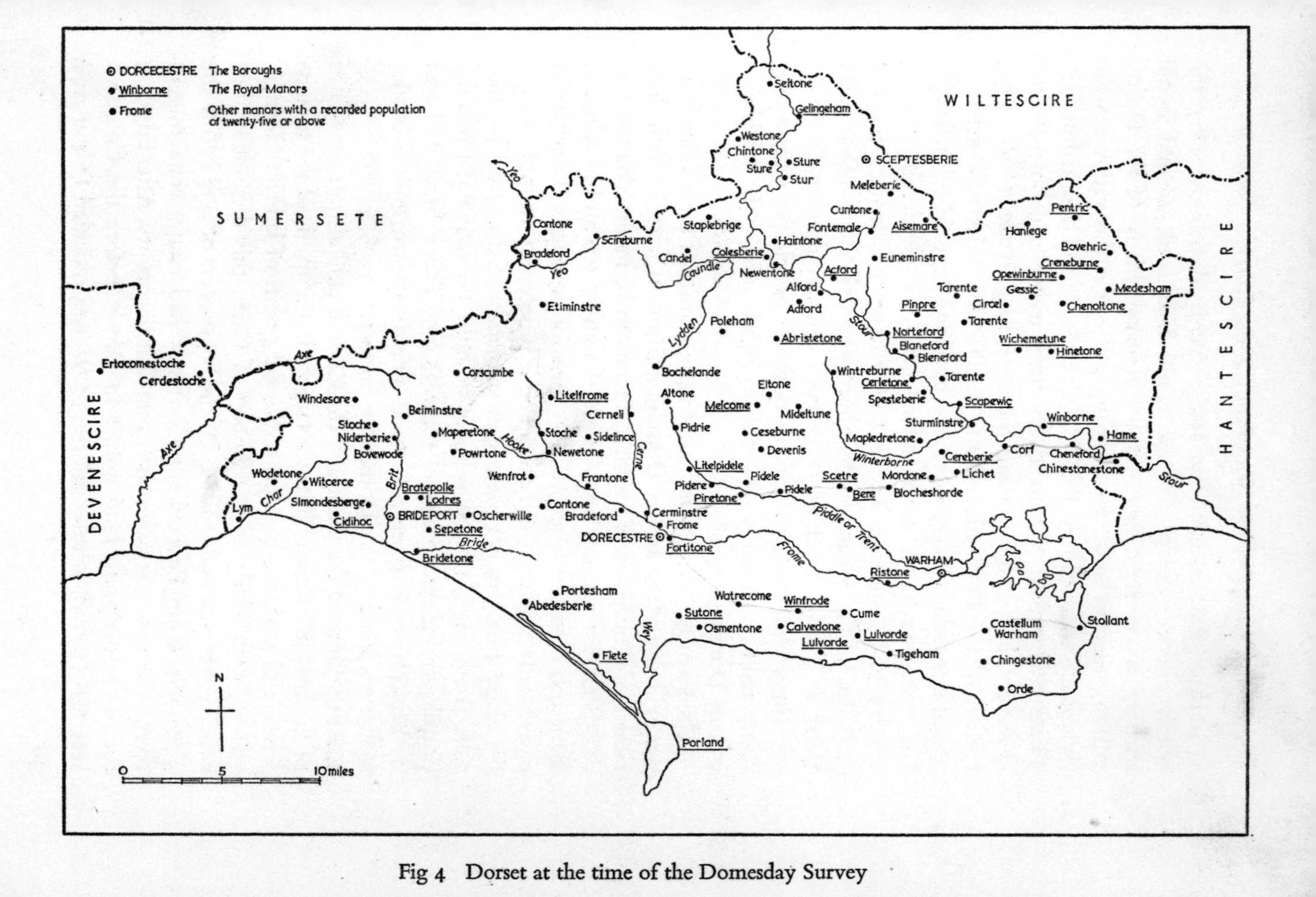

Fig 4 Dorset at the time of the Domesday Survey

Wareham. Settlements were fairly evenly distributed over the whole county, except for the sandy heathlands around Poole harbour where settlement was very sparse. Many of the Dorset villages, then as now, were strung out along the valleys of the rivers such as the Frome, the Piddle, the Stour and their tributaries. These villages had comparatively little arable land but used the chalk downlands for grazing the very large flocks of sheep recorded in the Domesday Book. In the clay vales of north and west Dorset the villages were much more irregularly distributed. Here there was much more arable land and a considerably greater density of population. There were also very extensive areas of woodland. The area around Sherborne is revealed in the Domesday Book as clearly the most prosperous and populous in Dorset at this time, with a population of some ten people per square mile compared to less than four people per square mile in the heathlands of east Dorset.

The attempt to calculate the total population of the county from the evidence given in the Domesday Book is fraught with difficulties, and only a very rough estimate can be made. The Domesday Book lists a rural population of some 7,500 and in addition some 600 persons are recorded in the four boroughs. These are of course only the heads of houses and it is necessary to multiply the figure by 4 or 5 to get some approximation of the actual population. Assuming 4 + persons per household we arrive at a population figure for the county of some 35,000. This is likely to be an underestimate, however, since, as already shown, not all settlements are listed in the Domesday Survey.

At the time of the Conquest the Church held almost two-fifths of the land in Dorset. This was largely in the hands of the monasteries, and apart from some additional grants of land to Norman abbeys, particularly to the Abbey of Caen, this did not change much in the years after 1066. Of the lay owners of land before the Conquest, King Edward the Confessor had estates consisting of twenty-one manors scattered throughout the county. After Edward, the most important land holder in Dorset before the Conquest was Earl Harold, whose earldom of Wessex included Dorset, and who held about one-eighth of the land of Dorset held by laymen, excluding the king. His estates included the large and important manor of Puddletown. Another important pre-Conquest land holder was Beorhtric, son of Aelfgar, whose lands included the manors of Cranborne, Ashmore, Frome St Quintin, Tarrant Launceston and Tyneham. Below these were a large number of lesser English landowners. The Norman Conquest resulted in a vast redistribution of lands in Dorset as elsewhere. The possessions of the religious houses suffered no major upset, but only a few other landowners survived the Conquest undisturbed. In 1086 the king remained the largest single landowner, having taken over the manors previously held by Edward the Confessor and by Earl Harold. After the king the greatest landowner in Dorset was Robert, count of Mortain, the king's half-brother, whose Dorset lands were only a small part of his vast estates. Most of the rest of Dorset was held by Norman barons, with only a few Englishmen remaining in possession of small estates. In addition, manors were distributed by the king to minor officials such as huntsmen, chamberlains, ushers, etc.

Of the lands listed as belonging to the Church in 1086, by far the greater part were in the hands of the bishop of Salisbury. Between 1075 and 1078 the bishopric of Sherborne was transferred to the larger and more populous town of Salisbury, so that in 1086 the extensive endowments of the former bishop of Sherborne belonged to the new see of Salisbury. The church lands also included the estates of the great nunnery of Shaftesbury, the largest nunnery in England, and the possessions of the monasteries of Sherborne, Cerne, Milton, Abbotsbury, Cranborne and Horton. In addition, several monasteries outside Dorset, particularly Glastonbury and Winchester, possessed lands in the county.

Parish churches are not mentioned in the Domesday Survey except incidentally, and only twelve places are referred to as having churches. There is little doubt, however, that considerably more churches already existed, since the list of places mentioned as having churches does not include many of those which are known to have possessed minster churches at this date. Oddly enough the existence of a market is not mentioned at any of the four towns. Each of the boroughs, however, possessed an essential element for any town engaged in trading activities—a mint. The Survey recorded that in 1066 there had been one moneyer at Bridport, two each at Dorchester and Wareham, and three at Shaftesbury. No mention is made of the position in 1086, but coins from all four boroughs were struck during the reigns of William the Conqueror and William Rufus. A fifth place in Dorset may perhaps be described as a town at this time. This is Wimborne Minster, which although it is not classed as a borough in the Domesday Book, is said to have had burgesses, and may perhaps have had a market.

There had been a great deal of destruction at all four boroughs, the consequence no doubt of the troubles and resistance following the Conquest. Of the 172 houses in Dorchester in 1066 only 88 remained standing in 1086. The same situation prevailed in the other boroughs, Wareham had only 135 houses left standing and 150 had been destroyed, in Shaftesbury 61 houses had been destroyed and 177 remained, Bridport had 100 houses remaining and 20 had gone. The only explanation for this large-scale destruction is the havoc wrought by the Norman army passing through the county on its way to besiege Exeter in 1068, and the continuing resistance to Norman rule in Dorset which continued for a few years after the Conquest. According to Domesday the damage is said to have been caused during the time that Hugh Fitz Grip was sheriff. He had become sheriff immediately after the Conquest and was no doubt concerned to suppress ruthlessly any sign of resistance to Norman rule.

Any attempt to calculate the populations of these boroughs in 1086 from the figures given in Domesday must of necessity be very speculative, but a recent attempt to do so has produced the following figures for the populations of the four towns:

Shaftesbury	1,000 people
Dorchester	700 people
Wareham	700 people
Bridport	500 people

Wimborne Minster was a good deal smaller than the other towns, and probably had a population of about 400.

No less than 276 mills are recorded, concentrated of course in the river valleys. There were twelve at Dorchester, twelve at Sherborne, eight at Burton Bradstock and eight at Wimborne. Salt pans and salt workers are mentioned at Studland, Ower, in the Weymouth area and at Lyme Regis. Fishermen are mentioned at Lyme Regis and in the Weymouth area. There were vineyards at Durweston and Wootton and appropriately an orchard is recorded at Orchard. The Exeter text of the Domesday Survey gives details concerning livestock on the various manors, but unfortunately this text only includes 160 of the 515 manors of Dorset. It is obvious that sheep were already of outstanding importance in the agriculture of the county, and some very large flocks are recorded. On the royal manors for example there were 1,037 sheep at Cranborne, 1,600 at Puddletown, 900 at Portland, and 800 at Burton Bradstock.

The pattern of landholding in the county at the time of the Domesday Survey illustrates very clearly the predominance of large estates in the county and the way in which the royal and ecclesiastical lands far out-numbered the estates of other landowners. The map on page 35 shows all the royal manors in the county, as well as all the other estates which are shown in the Survey as having a recorded population of more than twenty-five. It should be noted that this figure includes only heads of households and has to be multiplied by four or five times to give the approximate total population. In addition to the manors shown on the map there were some two hundred other manors listed in the Survey. These have been omitted either because they had a recorded population of less than twenty-five, or because their sites cannot now be identified. There were many small manors in the clay vales of west Dorset, the valleys of the Stour and Frome, in the area to the south and west of Dorchester and in the Isle of Purbeck. A few very large manors such as Sherborne, Portland or Puddletown included much of their surrounding areas. These facts explain some of the apparently empty areas on the map.

The heathland to the north and north-west of Wareham was very thinly populated at the time of the Domesday Survey and for many centuries thereafter. Many of the royal manors are recorded together in the Survey and for many of them it is not possible to arrive at a figure for their recorded population. All the royal manors, irrespective of their recorded population, have therefore been shown on the map. Finally it should be noted that the county boundary shown on the map shows the changes which were made during the nineteenth and early twentieth centuries. Thus Stockland (Ertacomestoche) and Chardstock (Cerdestoche) which were formerly in Dorset are shown in Devon and Kinson (Chinestanestone) in Hampshire.

SELECT BIBLIOGRAPHY

H. C. Darby and R. W. Finn	*The Domesday Geography of South-West England* (1967)
A. Fagërsten	*The Place Names of Dorset* (1933)
G. B. Grundy	'Saxon Charters of Dorset' (*Dorset Proceedings*, vol 55, 1933—vol 61, 1939)
W. G. Hoskins	*The Westward Expansion of Wessex* (1960)
C. F. C. Hawkes	'Britons, Romans and Saxons in Cranborne Chase' (*Archaeological Journal*, vol 104, 1947)
K. Jackson	'The Site of Mount Badon' (*Journal of Celtic Studies*, December 1958)
Victoria County History	*Dorset*, vol I (1908); vol III (1968)

Chapter 3 AGRICULTURE AND THE LAND

Agriculture has always been of supreme importance in the economy of Dorset, and until very recent times the great majority of the inhabitants of the county made their living directly from the land. It is clear that by the time of the Domesday Survey in 1086 the main pattern of settlement in Dorset was already established. Dorset was always essentially a county of small scattered rural communities, and large villages and towns were very much the exception. At the time of the Survey, there still remained large areas of waste, forest and heathland. There was also a very considerable area of royal forest in which settlement was limited or expansion restricted, such as the royal forest of Blackmoor which covered most of the Vale of Blackmoor, or the forests of Gillingham and Purbeck, as well as the large area of Cranborne Chase. It is some indication of the nature of this forest and waste land that wolves were still to be found there as late as the thirteenth century. In 1210 two huntsmen at Gillingham were rewarded by King John for killing two wolves in the forest, though perhaps the fact that they were given as much as 15s suggests that it was an unusual incident. There was certainly ample scope for expansion and for the founding of new farms and settlements, in the heathlands of the south-east and south, in the heavily wooded claylands of the north and west of the county and in the chalk areas of central Dorset where cultivation could be extended up the hillsides by the formation of strip-lynchets, the remains of which can still be seen in many places. During the twelfth and thirteenth centuries the pressure of increasing population led to expansion in all these areas. This period witnessed a massive increase in the cultivated area and a steady growth of single farmsteads each carved laboriously out of untamed heath or forest land by the hard pioneering toil of several generations of Dorset farmers.

Evidence of this process of expansion during the twelfth and thirteenth centuries comes from all over the county, and from a variety of sources. Apart from the evidence of the strip-lynchets which occur so widely in the county, there are throughout the clay areas vast numbers of the small irregularly shaped fields which are the typical result of forest clearing enclosure during the Middle Ages. This is particularly true of large areas of the Marshwood Vale where the small fields are enclosed by massive winding hedges and there are many isolated farms incorporating 'hay', meaning 'enclosure', in their names as further evidence of their origin. In the Blackmoor Vale many field names incorporate the element 'hay', particularly around Gillingham, Motcombe and Sherborne.

Further evidence of expansion and population growth is seen in the increase in the number of tithings assessed for taxation. In the subsidy rolls of 1327 and 1332 the hundred of Whitchurch Canonicorum in the Marshwood Vale is shown as having only four tithings; by the end of the medieval period the number had risen to no fewer than eighteen. At Beaminster the tithings of Wambrook and Bowood appear, and there was similar expansion elsewhere, for example in the hundreds of Sturminster Newton, Badbury and Cranborne. The overwhelming impression, particularly of the thirteenth century, is of massive expansion of settlement and clearance of woodland and waste.

Another interesting piece of documentary evidence for growth and development during the twelfth century occurs in two detailed surveys made of the lands of Shaftesbury Abbey, the first dating from about 1130–5 and the second from a generation or so later, about 1170–80. One of the estates of the abbey was Fontmell Magna and the earlier survey lists 65 tenants, including 22 villeins each holding a yardland and 19 villeins each holding half a yardland, the others were cottagers farming various amounts of land, generally about 4 acres. There were 4 mills listed in the survey of c. 1130, and this in itself is some evidence of growth since the Domesday Survey records 3 mills. By the time of the second survey it is clear that the population of the village has risen and the amount of cultivated land has increased considerably. There were now no fewer than 80 tenants, 28 villeins each with a yardland and 27 with half a yardland, and there were still 4 mills in the village.

By about the end of the twelfth century, the Dorset landscape had already taken on something of its appearance today. Christopher Taylor, in his study of the Dorset landscape, concludes that 'By 1300 the landscape of Dorset was more extensively occupied, cultivated and grazed than ever before. Nowhere in the county could one stand and view any scene without the imprint of man's work upon it.'

Whilst settlements in Dorset generally remained quite small, the county was, and continued to be, one of large landowners, many of them non-resident. This stamped a particular character upon both agriculture and society. The situation revealed in Domesday where a few large landowners dominated the county continued throughout the Middle Ages and after. The royal lands were the most extensive, followed closely by the lands of the religious houses. These included the great monasteries of Dorset such as Sherborne, Cerne, Milton and Abbotsbury, and the rich nunnery of Shaftesbury, the wealthiest religious foundation for women in the country, which, besides extensive properties outside Dorset, held lands at Compton Abbas, Handley, Gussage St Andrew, Tarrant, Iwerne Minster and Fontmell Magna. There were also a number of religious houses outside Dorset which held considerable property in the county. Among these, the most important was Glastonbury which possessed estates at Buckland Newton, Sturminster Newton and Plush. Other religious houses with lands in Dorset included the New Minster at Winchester which possessed Piddletrenthide, one of the largest Dorset manors, Athelney, Tewkesbury, Christ Church [Hants], Forde Abbey situated just across the border in Devon, and Wilton Abbey. The bishop of

Salisbury possessed very extensive estates in the county throughout the Middle Ages including the hundreds of Sherborne, Yetminster and Beaminster.

Lists prepared for the king in 1285 and 1303 give details of other large landholders in the county at the end of the thirteenth century, including among several others the earl of Gloucester who held the great hundred of Cranborne, John de Newburgh who possessed Winfrith and Henry de Lacy, earl of Lincoln, who held Blandford, Canford and Kingston. Several of the chief landowners in the county during the thirteenth century held their lands from the king in return for unusual services. Radulfus de Stepham held Bryanston from the king in return for providing a man with a bow without a bowstring, and an arrow without feathers, for the king's army. John Godwyne had half a hide of land in Purse Caundle in return for tending any of the king's hounds which were injured while the king was hunting in Blackmoor forest, and for contributing 1d per year towards the enclosing of the king's park at Gillingham. William Russell held Kingston Russell for the service of counting out the king's chessmen on Christmas Day, and John de Newburgh's service for his lands consisted of holding the silver basin of water for the king to wash his hands on his birthday.

MEDIEVAL FARMING PRACTICE

It is clear that as early as the Domesday Survey there was already considerable specialisation in Dorset agriculture, and this was to increase during the Middle Ages. Sheep were of overwhelming importance in the county's economy. The partial figures for Dorset livestock which survive in the Exeter Domesday record no fewer than 22,362 sheep on the lands of twelve landowners, and the Dorset flocks undoubtedly grew greatly in size during the Middle Ages. Much research remains to be done on medieval agriculture in Dorset, and much of what follows is necessarily based on a few great estates for which details have survived. The Dorset estates of Glastonbury Abbey at Buckland Newton and Sturminster Newton show, however, very clearly the continuing concentration on sheep in the early fourteenth century, and the surviving figures for other estates show a similar preponderance of sheep. The Bindon Abbey estates in c. 1330, for example, had flocks totalling no less than 7,000. As will be shown later, the sheep flocks continued to increase in size so that even larger numbers are recorded in the sixteenth century and after.

The main arable lands of the county were situated within the valleys of the chalklands, and most of the land in these areas throughout the Middle Ages was cultivated in common fields, generally under a three-field system. Wheat, barley and oats were grown as well as mixed corn. On the Glastonbury estates wheat was the chief crop, possibly because it was transported to Glastonbury for consumption at the abbey. There was considerable small-scale interchange of products among neighbouring manors, and goods from outside the county changed hands at the markets and fairs which will be described later. Mills were naturally of great importance in the manorial economy and watermills were to be found all over Dorset, though there were few windmills. In details of manorial life, Dorset does not differ markedly from the well known features of medieval existence to be found elsewhere in England during this period.

THE LATER MIDDLE AGES

In the later Middle Ages, the fourteenth and fifteenth centuries, there was a marked decline in the prosperity of Dorset, and a notable contraction of the cultivated area. This was particularly the case on the chalklands where the evidence of a great many deserted settlements remain as witness of the abandonment of previously thriving communities. There are many examples of this process of contraction in the county. A good illustration may be found in the Piddle Valley where the evidences of abandoned settlements survive all down the valley. Many of these settlements had in the earlier Middle Ages been thriving communities, such as Waterston, Little Piddle or Bardolfston, which either disappeared completely or shrank to a tiny hamlet or single farmstead.

The reasons for this curiously marked decline and contraction are far from clear. Changes in soil fertility, in the available water supplies and possibly in the climate may have played a part. There can be little doubt, however, that a major factor was plague. The Black Death of the mid-fourteenth century began in Dorset, having travelled across Europe from the East. Most contemporary chronicles of the 'Great Pestilence' suggest that it entered England through the port of Melcombe Regis in July 1348, whence it spread rapidly through the kingdom. The plague was, then, continuously active in Dorset throughout the autumn of 1348 and during 1349. Some indication of the death roll from this particularly virulent disease may be gained from the unusually large numbers of vacant benefices in the diocese of Salisbury, which included Dorset, during this period. Unfortunately the episcopal registers are not co plete for the whole of the plague period, but it is clear that as many as half the benefices in the county were made vacant during the two years following the first onslaught of the plague. In March 1349 the Salisbury episcopal registers record an average of as many as two institutions a day to vacant benefices. In Bridport where there were normally two town bailiffs each year, four held office during the year 1349–50 '*in tempore Pestilentiae*'. Geoffrey Baker's chronicle written at this time records that the plague 'almost stripped the seaports of Dorset of their inhabitants'. As early as July 1349 the Calendar of Fine Rolls records that the king took note of the fact that in the prebends of Bere and Charminster 'the mortality of men in the present pestilence is so great that the lands thereof be untilled and the profits are lost'. Later, in 1352 the king ordered that all the men on the island of Portland should stay there for its safe-keeping and that no crops or victuals should be drawn out of the island because it was 'so depopulated on account of the late mortality in the time of the pestilence that the men left there will not be sufficient to defend the same against attacks'. Conditions remained bad on the island, since a similar order was made in 1371.

In 1381 there was a further serious epidemic in Dorset and the abbess and convent of Shaftesbury petitioned the king in Parliament for relief from taxation and other burdens on the grounds that because of the pestilence nearly all the tenants on their estates were dead, as well as cattle 'of great number and value' which had died also, not only at one place but on all their estates. This petition was granted by the Crown.

Further evidence of the economic decline and depopulation of the later Middle Ages is also seen in the ruinous condition of many properties described in the Inquisitions Post Mortem of these years. The very valuable account of the possession of Richard de Osmyngton, abbot of Cerne of 1356 lists 'divers buildings in ruin' at 'Radepol, Wyrdesforde, Affepuddle, Blokesworth and Wynfryd'. There are many similar references. In view of the comparative wealth of evidence on this subject the remark in the *Victoria County History*, vol II, published in 1908, that 'there is but little evidence of the extent of the ravages of the plague in the middle of the fourteenth century' in Dorset, needs to be considerably modified. Another reason for the depressed state of some coastal areas in Dorset was because of French attacks upon the coast, and evidence of intermittent attacks and enemy landings occurs throughout the period.

A major result of the contraction of the later Middle Ages in Dorset was a very great increase in sheep farming at the expense of arable land. These were the years in which the really enormous flocks of sheep made their appearance in the county, and were remarked upon by all travellers in the county during the sixteenth and seventeenth centuries and later. Some indication of the size of these flocks can be obtained from the details of each of the Dorset monasteries given in the Valor Ecclesiasticus, the great survey of Church property taken in 1535, on the eve of the dissolution of the monasteries. The entries for the Dorset monasteries in the Valor Ecclesiasticus are unique in that they describe the farming activities of the monasteries in some detail and in particular they give the figures for the numbers of sheep possessed by each monastery. The seven great monastic houses of Dorset, Abbotsbury, Bindon, Cerne, Milton, Shaftesbury, Sherborne and Tarrant Crawford possessed between them no less than 25,093 sheep. Milton Abbey situated in the centre of the chalklands was the largest sheep owner with 1,775 sheep at Milton and a further 5,554 sheep on outlying manors. Cerne came next with no fewer than 6,009 sheep scattered over the various monastic estates. The smallest flock, 885 sheep, was possessed by Sherborne Abbey whose estates lay generally in the claylands of the Blackmoor Vale.

Vast numbers of sheep were also kept by lay landowners, and the Probate Inventories of the sixteenth and seventeenth centuries often show surprisingly large numbers of sheep belonging to men who were obviously farming small arable acreages but who must clearly have had grazing rights over large areas of downland. Such flocks of course required a vast amount of land for grazing, and it is the profitability of sheep farming that led to the enclosure for permanent pasture that took place in many places in Dorset during the fifteenth century and later. Such enclosures often bore harshly on the poor, and it is significant that it was a Dorset man, Thomas Bastard, who was the author of the well known sixteenth-century rhyme:

> Sheepe have eate up our medows and our downes,
> Our Corne, our wood, whole villages and townes;
> Yes, they have eate up many wealthy men,
> Besides widowes and orphan children;
> Besides our statutes and our Iron Lawes,
> Which they have swallowed down into their mawes:
> Till now I thought the proverb did but jest,
> Which said a blacke sheepe was a biting beast.

THE CHANGES OF THE SIXTEENTH AND SEVENTEENTH CENTURIES

The economic and social changes of the sixteenth century, and in particular the dissolution of the monasteries led to the emergence of a large number of new landowning families. Out of 211 leading Dorset families in 1634 nearly half appear for the first time between 1529 and 1603. Some of these families rose from the ranks of yeoman tenant farmers grasping the opportunities for enrichment offered by the economic changes of the sixteenth century, others acquired land in the county by purchase or marriage.

A further important change was in the spread of enclosures in order more adequately to cope with the growing numbers of sheep. The sixteenth and seventeenth centuries saw a great deal of enclosure both of downland pasture and of former arable fields. At Iwerne Courtney, which belonged to the earls of Devon, a survey of the manor conducted in 1553, records that the lands were formerly in common, but that in 1548 the tenants had agreed among themselves and with the lord of the manor to enclose the land into separate holdings:

> The custumarye tenaunts were so small and so lyttle londe longinge to them that the tenaunts were not able to paye the lordes rent, but the one halfe of them departed the towne, and yielded up ther copies into the lordes handes; . . . and then every tenaunte inclosed his owne londes, so as the more parte of t' hole mannor was inclosed, and every tenaunt and fermor occupyed his grounde severall to hymself . . .

Similar enclosures by agreement, both of downland and of common fields, occurred all over Dorset, though documentary evidence for all of them does not survive. At Hinton St Mary for example almost half the fields had been enclosed by the last years of the sixteenth century, and enclosures for pasture had been carried out at Long Bredy, Gillingham, Motcombe, Beaminster, Cheddington and Charminster. During the seventeenth century the process continued and, among others, there were enclosures by agreement at North Poorton, South Mapperton where so many of the tenants died of the plague in 1665–6 that the lands were thrown together, and at West Parley and West Moors where there was a particularly interesting and unusual enclosure of heathland in 1633 whereby each tenant was given a long narrow allotment of land stretching right across the parish, nearly two miles long in order to ensure an equitable distribution of land of diverse quality.

Side by side with new ownership of the land, new methods of tenure and a much more profit-conscious approach to agriculture, went new crops and technical innovations, though these often remained the experiments of a few go-ahead farmers rather than the generally accepted practice. Among the crops were woad, hemp and flax, the last two in particular being produced in the rich soils of the Blackmoor Vale and west Dorset and finding a market in the rope walks of Bridport and the sailcloth industry of Beaminster, Crewkerne and district. Introductions included cabbages which were being grown by Sir Anthony Ashley at Wimborne St Giles in the 1660s, and clover and artificial grasses for the improvement of hay.

The most notable technical innovation in agricultural practice during this period was the introduction of water meadows. These did not originate in Dorset but they rapidly became extremely popular along the valleys of the Frome, Piddle and other suitable streams and have been described as 'the crowning glory of agricultural technique' from the seventeenth to the nineteenth centuries. The object of the water meadows was to flood the meadows by a complicated network of small water channels which were allowed to overflow at certain times and thus encourage a much earlier growth of grass which could be used for livestock feed in the most difficult time of the year, the early spring, when the winter feed had been eaten and the grass would not normally be ready for feeding. To construct a water meadow involved a most complex system of dams and channels and to produce the best results became a highly skilled job. The introduction of water meadows in Dorset has generally been ascribed to the seventeenth century, though it is probable that rudimentary methods of controlling the variable flow of the chalk streams were already being used long before, possibly with the idea of enhancing the fertility of the meadows or encouraging earlier growth of grass. The Calendar of Patent Rolls records a case in July 1362 against a number of persons who entered the lands belonging to the abbot of Abbotsbury at Tolpuddle and 'broke a stank lately erected by him of piles and timber to store water to flood his meadow with in time of summer and drought . . .'

The construction of water meadows with their complex system of channels for controlled flooding may, however, have begun at Puddletown shortly before 1629 when it was agreed at the manorial court there that the work already begun by some tenants of making watercourses for 'wateringe and improvinge theire groundes' should be continued. The advantages of water meadows were very rapidly apparent, and during the next few years the system was adopted by a number of places particularly in the Frome and Piddle Valleys and including Moreton, Winfrith Newburgh, Bovington, Tolpuddle, Affpuddle, etc. By the eighteenth century water meadows had become a common feature of the Dorset scene in those parts of the county where the valleys could be adapted for this purpose, and Stevenson in his *General View of the Agriculture of Dorset*, prepared in 1812, estimated that 'About 6,000 acres of meadow land in the chalky and sandy districts are regularly irrigated.' Apart from the rapid spread of water meadows along the valleys, the other important agricultural advance in Dorset during the sixteenth and seventeenth centuries was the large-scale reclamation of waste land. The wealth to be made from agriculture, particularly during the period from the defeat of the Armada to the outbreak of the Civil War, led to a demand for land which was met by considerably speeding up the immemorial process of clearing and enclosing the waste land, heath, forest and downs. The most spectacular example of this is the enclosure of Gillingham Forest. This ancient royal forest was finally disafforested in 1628, and the subsequent events there illustrate very clearly that the commoners did not always acquiesce in the destruction of their common rights even though their resistance generally proved ineffectual. In 1628 the lands at Gillingham were granted by Charles I to his former tutor Sir James Fullerton and to Mr George Kirke. Fullerton and Kirke then began to enclose the area to the intense annoyance of the commoners who immediately set upon the men making the enclosures and pulled down the fences. The dispute continued for several years, since the commoners held out for a long time proclaiming in splendidly independent fashion 'here we were born and here we stay'. Troops had eventually to be moved into the area to drive the commoners off their ancient lands, and the whole story emerges from the records of the Court of Star Chamber where eighty persons were fined and censured in

1629 for their part in the affair. The incident is particularly interesting both as an example of an attitude of sturdy though useless independence, and also as illustrating the opposition to enclosures among some sections of the community which no doubt existed elsewhere in Dorset but to which the surviving records do not bear witness.

DEVELOPMENTS DURING THE EIGHTEENTH AND NINETEENTH CENTURIES

There were great changes in Dorset agriculture, under the twin impetus of several energetic and improving landlords, and of the high prices of agricultural products during the long period of the Napoleonic Wars. A good example of the Dorset landlords who interested themselves in agriculture and in the improvement of their estates during the eighteenth century, was Humphrey Sturt of Crichel, a man of immense energy and full of enthusiasm for 'improvement' in agriculture. Among a great multitude of other projects, Sturt made a remarkable improvement in Brownsea Island in Poole harbour. Here he burnt off the heath and experimented with a variety of different crops, employing ships and barges to bring in manure from Poole, Portsmouth and even London. Sturt also carried out tremendous improvements on his estate at Crichel, greatly increased the size of the house there, and even moved the whole village of Moor Crichel to a new site some way to the south.

Improvements were also made by the Framptons at Moreton, particularly in the development of water meadows along the rivers Frome and Piddle, for which the estate was particularly well placed. In 1779 George Boswell of Puddletown published his *Treatise on Watering Meadows* and this had considerable influence in Dorset, giving detailed instructions for the creation and management of the intricate system of water channels which were necessary for a satisfactory water meadow.

Dedicated improvers during the eighteenth century like Sturt, Frampton, John Damer of Came, Viscount Milton of Milton Abbas, who is generally remembered only because he demolished the town of Milton Abbas to make way for a park around his house, and a great many others did a great deal to alter the whole character and landscape of large areas of Dorset, particularly in east Dorset. However, as pointed out earlier, it is necessary to beware of generalisations about Dorset agriculture in view of the very varied soil, climatic and other conditions of the county. Improved agriculture certainly did not affect the whole county during the eighteenth century. An objective observer of the agricultural scene was William Marshall whose *Rural Economy of the West of England* was published in 1796. Unfortunately Marshall only wrote about the western part of Dorset, in the neighbourhood of Bridport, but he was very disappointed by the agricultural standards he saw there. In this area of small farms and ancient enclosures Marshall commented on the poor quality of the grassland, overrun with weeds, on the water-logged ditches and on the general need for improved practices. In particular he strongly criticised the common Dorset practice of this time of farmers hiring out their cows to a dairyman, a system which he thought destroyed all incentive to improvement.

It is also clear from the few surviving Dorset returns to the Home Office inquiry of 1801 concerning arable crops in each parish, that the arable farming in many parts of Dorset was very backward, even after a number of years of high corn prices when improvement would have been very profitable. The return for Cerne Abbas for example mentions the common practice of fallowing which survived in the county: 'The land arable commonly rests here every fourth year, as it does in most parts of the county of Dorset.' At Sydling St Nicholas it was also reported that 'The Common Practice is to give the Land Rest every fourth year'.

On the Island of Portland, where the common arable fields have survived to the present day, half the land was left fallow each year. On Portland this was said to be partly due to lack of sufficient manure, since there were scarcely any trees on the island and dried dung was therefore used as fuel, though the practice of using dung as fuel was not unknown elsewhere in Dorset. William

Barnes, the poet who describes the Dorset rural scene during the nineteenth century so splendidly, mentions as part of a poem on the benefits of a common that:

> An when the children be too young to earn
> A penny, they can g'out in zunny weather,
> An' run about, an' get together
> A bag o' cow-dung vor to burn.

Nevertheless improvements did come. First in the huge extension of water meadows, which enabled more and more sheep to be kept. Secondly, the interest in obtaining larger returns from the land led in Dorset, as elsewhere, to the disappearance of the old open fields and downs in favour of enclosure. Most of the north and west of the county had already been enclosed before the eighteenth century or, having been won piecemeal from forest and waste over the centuries, had been enclosed from the first, and the eighteenth- and nineteenth-century enclosures affected mainly the chalklands. Great areas of chalk downland still remained unenclosed at the end of the eighteenth century. Claridge, in his *Survey of Dorset Agriculture* of 1793, writes lyrically that 'The most striking feature of the County is the open and uninclosed parts, covered by numerous flocks of sheep, scattered over the Downs . . .' Within the next few years these 'open and uninclosed parts' were mostly divided and separated by hedges. There was some enclosure of common arable fields, sometimes by Act of Parliament, as at Wyke Regis in 1797, Tolpuddle in 1794, Cattistock in 1807 or Piddletrenthide in 1817 and several other places. Others were enclosed by agreement among the tenants, for example at Cerne Abbas, where the extent of the former open fields can still be clearly seen from the superb viewpoint by the Giant, the land was enclosed into rectangular fields about 1800. Unlike many other parts of England, Parliamentary enclosure of common arable fields played only a fairly small part in Dorset enclosures. Far more important was the very widespread enclosure of downland and common which took place during the French War and continued during the nineteenth century. It was this aspect of enclosure, the consequent loss of common grazing rights and the decline in the numbers of small farms, which so impressed contemporaries. As Barnes put it:

> Then ten good dearies (dairies) were a-ved
> Along that water's winden bed,
> An' in the lewth o' hills an' wood
> A half a score farm-housen stood:
> But now—count all o'm how you would,
> So many less do hold the land—
> You'd vind but vive that still do stand,
> A' comen down vrom gramfers.

Proposals for enclosure were not of course always successful. A sustained attempt by some of the larger landowners to secure the enclosure of the large manor of Fordington which lasted from 1801 to 1814 was frustrated by the concerted opposition of the tenants of smallholdings, and enclosure was postponed until 1876. Likewise all attempts to enclose the open arable fields of the Island of Portland foundered on the reluctance of the large number of freehold tenants of this royal manor to allow any change, and the fields there remain to this day.

The ending of the French Wars and the consequent depression brought a severe check to the progress of agriculture in Dorset. Many tenant farmers who had made large outlays of capital in the expectation of continuing high prices, failed in the hard times which followed the war. Between 1815 and 1820 alone, fifty-two farmers cultivating between them 24,000 acres failed in Dorset, and a great many more gave up farming. These years also of course saw a very great deal of suffering and privation among the farm labourers in Dorset culminating in the Riots of 1830 and the severely repressive measures which followed. This will be discussed in chapter 8.

By the 1840s however agriculture was once more prosperous, and Louis H. Ruegg, the editor of a local paper, in an essay on the *Farming of Dorsetshire* published by the Royal Agricultural Society in 1854 claimed that the standard of farming in much of the county was as high as any in England: 'from Woodyates to six miles beyond Dorchester (nearly the entire length of the chalk district) there is no better farming in the Kingdom.' Ruegg, like other writers of the mid-nineteenth century, also comments on the thousands of acres of downland still being brought under cultivation, and mentions, for example, 2,000 acres of downland ploughed up in the neighbourhood of Cerne Abbas during the previous ten years, or the whole district between Bryanston and Milton Abbas which had been brought under cultivation. 'Between Dorchester and Blandford there is scarcely a parish in which downs have not been broken up.'

The first detailed statistics concerning the distribution of landed property in Dorset since the Domesday Book are given in the *Return of the Owners of Land* made to Parliament in 1873. This gives a splendid picture of the landowning class in Dorset at the height of its power and opulence, before the depression of agriculture in the later nineteenth century. As in the Domesday Survey of 1087, Dorset is shown to be a county where vast estates predominated. Dorset was fourth among the English counties in the total proportion of its area occupied by estates of more than 10,000 acres. Thirty-six per cent of Dorset was part of such enormous estates as against a national average of 24 per cent. There were in the county 3,409 owners of land of above one acre in extent and between them they owned 571,757 acres. These owners included 10 'Peers' possessing a total of 122,625 acres and 24 'Great Landowners' who owned at least 3,000 acres each. In addition there were 59 'Squires' each with estates of between 1,000 and 3,000 acres.

Among the largest landowners in the county were the following with estates of more than 10,000 acres, though it must be remembered that this list does not include several landowners such as, for example, Sir Henry Hoare, Lord Portman or the Cecils, the bulk of whose estates lay in other counties. It must also be noted that those listed often also possessed very large estates elsewhere.

Landowner	*Principal residence in the County*	*Acreage in the County*
Lord Rivers	Rushmore	24,942
George Digby Wingfield Digby	Sherborne Castle	21,451
Earl of Ilchester	Melbury House	15,981
Earl of Shaftesbury	Wimborne St Giles	15,579[1]
Edward J. Weld	Lulworth Castle	15,478
Henry G. Sturt	Crichel	14,211
Sir Ivor Guest	Canford	12,930
Richard Brinsley Sheridan	Frampton Court	11,468
Walter Ralph Bankes	Kingston Lacy	10,675[2]

[1] This figure is corrected in J. Bateman, *The Great Landowners of Great Britain* (1883), to 17,317 acres.

[2] This figure is corrected by Bateman to 19,228.

The number of large estates in the county was as follows:

Size of Estate (acres)	*Number of Owners*
Over 10,000	9
5,000–10,000	13
1,000–5,000	98

The agricultural prosperity of Dorset ended abruptly and dismally with the farming depression which began in the late 1870s. The depression which lasted virtually until 1914 was marked by rapidly declining prices, and by very great hardship and distress among farmers. The price of corn fell dramatically. For example in 1847 wheat sold at 70s per quarter, by 1870 the price had fallen to 46s, and in 1894 it was 24s per quarter. There was also a similar fall in the price of livestock, and, for Dorset, a particularly serious and permanent fall in wool prices. Much of this drop in prices was of course due to the competition of cheap imported corn and foodstuffs. A similar fall in the price of flax in face of foreign competition led to a spectacular decline in the acreage devoted to this crop in Dorset. In 1881 there were 225 acres of flax grown in the county. By 1884 the number had fallen to 117 and by 1894 had slumped to a mere 25.

The effects of this depression in a county so dependent upon agriculture were naturally widespread and numerous. They are to be seen in the rapid decline of population in almost every town and village in Dorset between 1871 and 1901, as farmers reduced their labour force and many hundreds of men and often whole families were forced to seek work elsewhere, and in the decay of all those trades and occupations which depended upon agriculture. For example, at Cerne Abbas, the population fell from 1,164 in 1871 to 634 in 1901, and the hitherto prosperous trades of tanning, leatherworking and brewing which had long been carried on there, disappeared. Population statistics for some other widely scattered villages, taken as examples of the general trend, all tell the same story.

	1871	*1901*
Hazelbury Bryan	852	541
Beaminster	2,585	1,702
Long Bredy	1,115	741
North Poorton	88	42
Powerstock	1,061	631
Whitchurch Canonicorum	1,365	868
Buckland Newton	1,138	755
Cheselbourne	408	194

The depression also hit the landowners very badly, since inevitably rents had to be reduced or were not paid at all, so that the 1895 Commission reported of Dorset that, 'Ownership of agricultural land is rapidly becoming a luxury which only men possessing other sources of income can enjoy.' Farm buildings were neglected, land was laid down to grass, water meadows fell into disuse, cottages were untenanted, and markets and fairs, and even the traditional market dinners, 'the market ordinaries', declined or ceased. The sheep flocks were very badly hit by the fall in the price of wool, and the number of sheep kept in the county declined dramatically, and has never recovered. The number of sheep fell from about 500,000 in 1850, to 300,000 in 1900, and to 47,000 in 1947. Rider Haggard, who visited Dorset in 1901, wrote that 'From Yeovil to Dorchester, the capital of the county of Dorset . . . it is pasture, pasture all the way, scarcely relieved by the sight of a single piece of arable.'

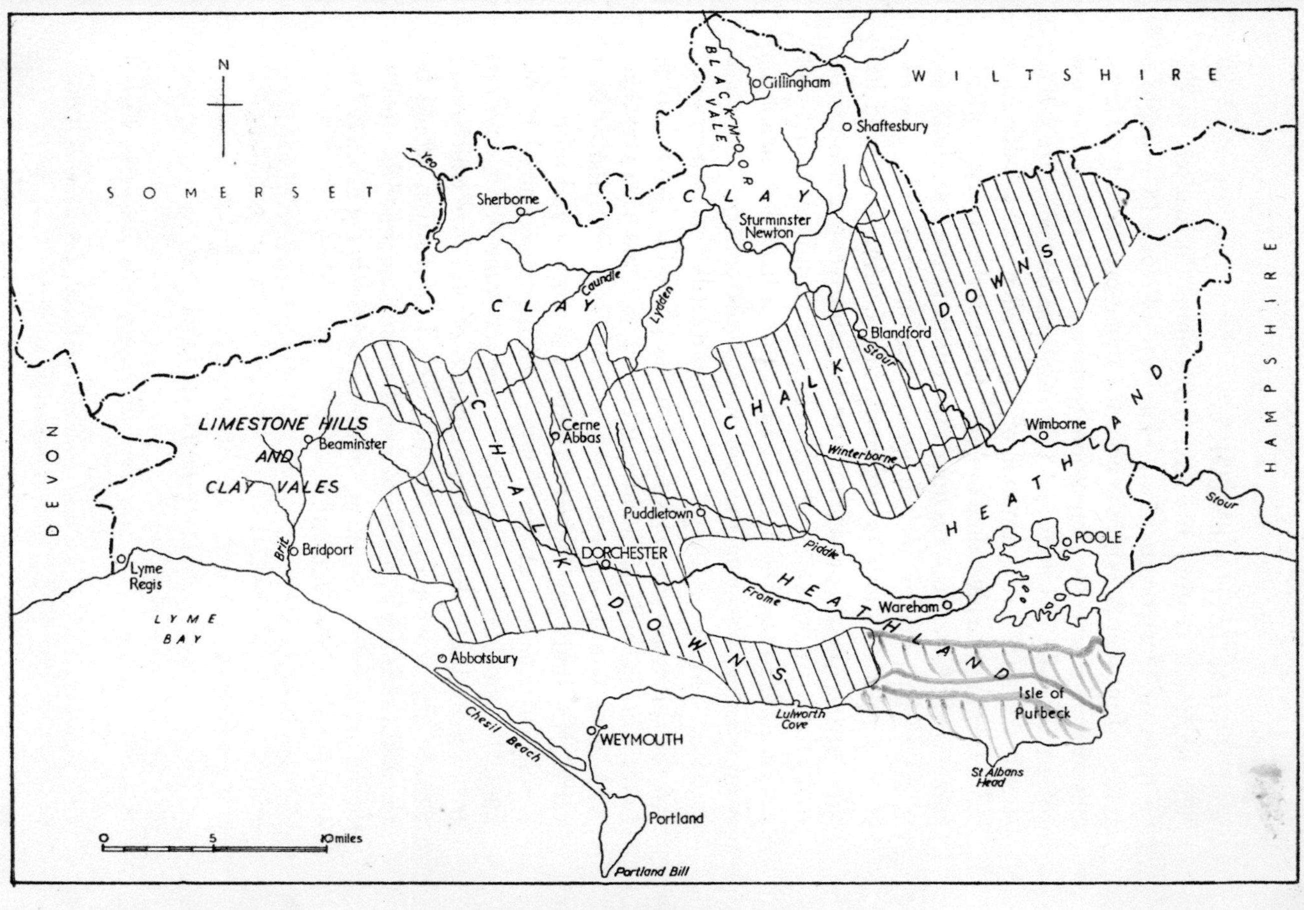

Fig 5 Agricultural regions of Dorset

THE TWENTIETH CENTURY

The twentieth century has seen tremendous fluctuations in the fortunes of Dorset agriculture. The war of 1914–18 brought a return of prosperity with the need for home-produced foodstuffs, but after the war the depression returned, and with it the old pattern of unlet holdings and vast areas put down to grass. The steady decrease in the amount of land under arable cultivation was of course sharply halted in 1939, and since then Dorset agriculture has developed in ways quite different from the past, under the impetus given by new techniques and machinery, and by government supported subsidies and marketing boards. The trend has been towards cereal production and the improvement and expansion of dairy farming. Sheep farming, the traditional standby of the Dorset farmer, has declined to a point where it is no longer of much importance in the economy of the county. The water meadows have gone out of use, and the chalklands which once fed the enormous flocks of sheep are now used to grow barley. In the Blackmoor Vale and in west Dorset there has been a tremendous expansion of dairy farming and of the production of beef cattle. No doubt the Dorset farmers of a century and more ago would be staggered at the changes which have occurred to the land, though they would perhaps recognise some of the developments as no more than the continuation of processes which were already old in their day. Possibly their first reaction would be less at the changes in the landscape, than amazement at the quality of the cattle and the excellence of the crops now being produced on the land they once farmed.

SELECT BIBLIOGRAPHY

H. C. Darby and R. W. Finn — *The Domesday Geography of South-West England* (1967)

G. E. Fussell — 'Four Centuries of Farming Systems in Dorset' (*Dorset Proceedings*, vol 73, 1952)

B. Kerr	*Bound to the Soil* (1968)
R.C.H.M.	*Dorset*
C. C. Taylor	*The Making of the English Landscape: Dorset* (1970) 'The Pattern of Medieval Settlement in the Forest of Blackmoor' (*Dorset Proceedings*, vol 87, 1966)
Victoria County History	*Dorset*, vol II (1908); vol III (1968)
B. J. Whitehead	'The Management and Land-Use of Water Meadows in the Frome Valley, Dorset' (*Dorset Proceedings*, vol 89, 1968)

Chapter 4 DORSET TOWNS

ALTHOUGH Dorset has always been predominantly an agricultural county, nonetheless its ports and market towns have had an extremely important role in its economy. There are in the county more than twenty-five places which have had at some time or another a claim to be called towns, besides nearly fifty places which have had fairs. The early history of the towns after the Roman occupation is as yet very obscure, and needs a great deal of detailed archaeological and other research before much can be said with certainty. The Burghal Hidage, a list of 'burhs' or fortified centres, not necessarily towns, dating from the early years of the tenth century, lists three 'burhs' in Dorset—Wareham, Shaftesbury and 'Bredy' which may be identified with a site in Little Bredy parish or, perhaps more plausibly, with Bridport. The Burghal Hidage list omits some places which are known to have been important, for example Dorchester, from where according to the *Anglo-Saxon Chronicle* the King's reeve rode out in 787 to enquire the business of the Danish raiders who had landed on Portland, or Sherborne which was already an important ecclesiastical centre at that time. Of the Dorset 'burhs', Wareham retains its defences most visibly, and the impressive earth banks and ditches there enclose an area of between eighty and ninety acres. These walls are a magnificent example of early town defences. The splendid Saxon minster church of Lady St Mary survived at Wareham until 1841, when in an incredible act of civic vandalism the whole of the nave was demolished and re-built. Beorhtric, king of Wessex was buried there in 802. Shaftesbury is also set in an imposing defensive situation on its hilltop, and there also an important minster church was established by the early eighth century. In the ninth century King Alfred established there the very richly endowed nunnery, with his daughter as abbess, and it was the burial place of King Edward the Martyr in 978, and soon became a very popular place of pilgrimage.

The Domesday Survey of 1086 as previously stated lists four Dorset boroughs, Dorchester, Wareham, Bridport and Shaftesbury. Wimborne Minster, another early minster site, seems also to have had some burgesses, and may be counted as a town at this time, though it is not listed as a borough. It is clear that these towns were not large, and that it was the possession of a market, burgesses, perhaps courts and possibly a mint, which distinguished them from the neighbouring villages. All the boroughs had suffered considerable destruction in the years following the Conquest, and some indication of this and of their relative sizes can be seen in the following table:

Borough	Number of houses in 1066	Number of houses destroyed	Number of houses standing in 1086	Assessment for geld	Amount paid in tax
DORCHESTER	172	100	88	10 Hides	1 Mark (13/4d)
WAREHAM	285	150	135	10 Hides	1 Mark (13/4d)
SHAFTESBURY	257	81	177	20 Hides	2 Marks (26/8d)
BRIDPORT	120	20	100	5 Hides	½ Mark (6/8d)

It is evident that Shaftesbury with its rich and important nunnery was considerably larger and more important than the other towns.

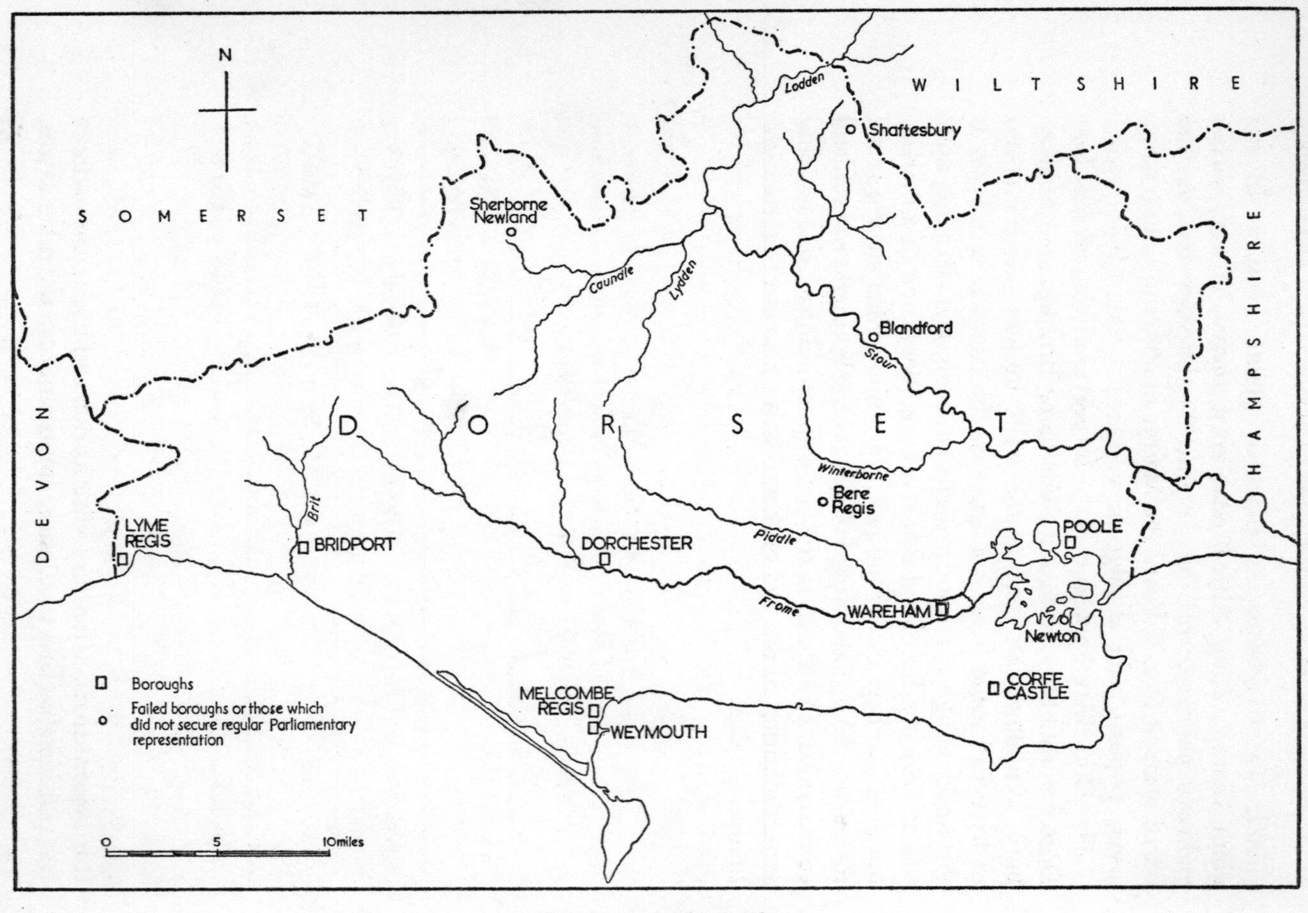

Fig 6 Dorset boroughs

In the twelfth and thirteenth centuries several new towns came into existence, as the lords of various manors sought to increase their revenue by encouraging the growth of towns and markets on their land. Thus a whole series of little market towns grew up, most of them serving purely local needs and remaining quite small. So small indeed, that today it is often difficult to appreciate the former importance of towns like Beaminster, Maiden Newton, Frampton, Evershot, Bere Regis or Cranborne. Other towns developed because of the existence of a great monastery, such as Abbotsbury, Cerne, Milton, Wool and to some extent Sherborne. Others grew because of royal encouragement or protection like Corfe or Gillingham, or because of their position on important routes like Cranborne or Blandford. Today the market places in towns such as Beaminster, Abbotsbury, Cerne or Cranborne are still clearly to be seen and bear witness to their former importance, even though later buildings have often been erected upon the site of the old stalls and booths.

There are a number of well documented examples of the deliberate establishment of new towns or new parts of older towns during the Middle Ages, though not all of them were successful. In 1227–8 the great bishop of Salisbury, Richard Poore, set up a new borough at Newland in the then arable fields adjacent to his existing town of Sherborne. This still exists as the single street of Newland, though it never achieved much success as a borough. At nearby Yetminster a weekly market and an annual three-day fair was established by the bishop of Salisbury in 1300. The fair continued to be held until the nineteenth century, but there is no evidence that the market ever prospered and Yetminster never rose beyond the status of a village. The best known example of the foundation of a completely new town in Dorset during the Middle Ages is also the most spectacularly unsuccessful. This was to be the town of Newton, on the southern shores of Poole harbour. Here in 1286, Edward I ordered a new town to be laid out, with a market place, fair, streets, church and a harbour, on a site owned by the king. From here he hoped that the export of Purbeck stone would take place, rather than from nearby Ower.

But the project was a complete failure. Perhaps because of the competition from Poole, perhaps because of the decline in the popularity of the Purbeck stone, the reason still is not certain. But scarcely any of Newton was built, and today the site remains as empty heathland with little or no indication on the ground to show the great future that was once projected for it.

The Middle Ages also saw the development of four major new ports in Dorset—Lyme Regis, Weymouth, Melcombe Regis and Poole—rivalling and soon surpassing the two older ports of Bridport and Wareham.

LYME REGIS

Lyme Regis owed its emergence as a port entirely to the construction of the remarkable breakwater known as the Cobb. This was built in the late thirteenth century and provided a protection for ships in that otherwise inhospitable and dangerous stretch of coastline. The maintenance of the Cobb was to prove a heavy burden, since it was constantly damaged by storms, but as a result of the harbour which it provided the town began to grow and prosper. By 1295 it gained a charter from Edward I and began sending representatives to Parliament. When Leland visited it in c. 1540 he described it as '. . . a praty market town, set in the rootes of an high rokky hille down to the hard shore. This town hath good shippes and usith fisshing and merchauntice. Merchauntes of Morleys in Britaine [Morlaix in Brittany] much haunt this town'.

WEYMOUTH AND MELCOMBE REGIS

There had been a Roman port and harbour at Radipole up the river estuary from the present towns of Weymouth and Melcombe Regis, but after the Roman period there was no port in the area until the thirteenth century, in spite of the good harbour which it provides. At the time of the Domesday Survey Radipole was no more than a small manor of Cerne Abbey, and there is no mention of any port. Both towns came into existence as ports in the middle years of the thirteenth century, Weymouth on the south bank of the river and Melcombe Regis, occupying the land to the north, between Radipole Lake and the sea. Both ports prospered greatly during the years before the Black Death of 1348–9, and became major exporters of wool; both were hit very badly by the plague, which started at Melcombe Regis and wrought havoc in the towns. Inevitably the two towns, facing each other across the narrow harbour, constantly quarrelled over shipping, harbour dues, justice and a host of other matters. The ill feeling continued until eventually in 1571 the towns were united by a charter, although they both continued to send two members to Parliament until 1832.

POOLE

Poole rose to prominence as a port during the thirteenth century as a consequence of the decline of the older port of Wareham. The first mention of a settlement at the edge of the great heath and common belonging to the parish of Canford, whose centre was nearly five miles inland, occurs in the late twelfth century. In c. 1248 Poole emerges as a town with a charter obtained by William Longespee, earl of Salisbury and lord of the manor of Canford. Poole prospered and grew rapidly, profiting from its splendid harbour and from the demand for Purbeck marble. By the mid-fourteenth century it had already overtaken Melcombe Regis in importance and had become the first port in the county. After a set-back caused by the Black Death in 1348–9, the growth of the port continued, and its importance was recognised in 1568 when it was granted a charter giving it the status of a county, with full jurisdiction over its internal affairs. The sixteenth century and later development of the town was based very largely on the fishing fleet specialising in cod from the distant Newfoundland grounds. This, together with the trade with Newfoundland which accompanied it, brought great wealth and prosperity to Poole. It far out-stripped the other Dorset towns, and today is far larger than any of them.

During the seventeenth century, apart from Poole, Dorchester and Sherborne were the two largest towns, both of them greatly dependent upon the cloth industry. Dorchester, because of its central position was the Assize town, but it was not yet the administrative centre of the county. Sherborne, though never a Parliamentary borough, was possibly of equal consequence in the life of the county. Thomas Gerard of Trent writing in c. 1633 noted of Dorchester, 'The inhabitants of this Place gaine much by Clotheing and altogether trade in Merchandise . . .' and commented on its 'quick Marketts and neate Buildings' and on its evident wealth. While of Sherborne, he wrote, 'This Towne for Largenesse, Frequencie of Inhabitants and quicke Marketts giveth place to none in these Partes'.

One factor in the development of Dorset towns which must not be overlooked is the frequency of disastrous fires which destroyed great parts of several of the towns. The best known example of this is the great fire at Blandford in 1731, which necessitated a complete rebuilding, much of it carried out in a splendid manner by two brothers John and William Bastard. Much of their work remains including the parish church (1739) and the Town Hall. But Blandford had already had three previous great fires in 1579, 1677 and 1713, and fire was a constant hazard throughout the county. Wood and thatch were used extensively in the houses, and there were severe fires for example at Dorchester in 1613, 1622, 1713, 1725 and 1775 and similarly frequent outbreaks elsewhere. The hooks for tearing the burning thatch from the roofs, which are still kept, for example at Bere Regis church, are a reminder of the ever-present danger which threatened all the towns and villages. The Quarter Sessions accounts and churchwardens records for parishes throughout the county, have many references to requests for help being made by people who 'have lost all by fire'.

One Dorset town was completely destroyed during the eighteenth century. This was Milton Abbas which had grown up round the important monastery, and after the dissolution had survived as a thriving busy market town serving the rich agricultural region of central Dorset. The town was completely demolished by Viscount Milton between 1771 and 1790 to clear the

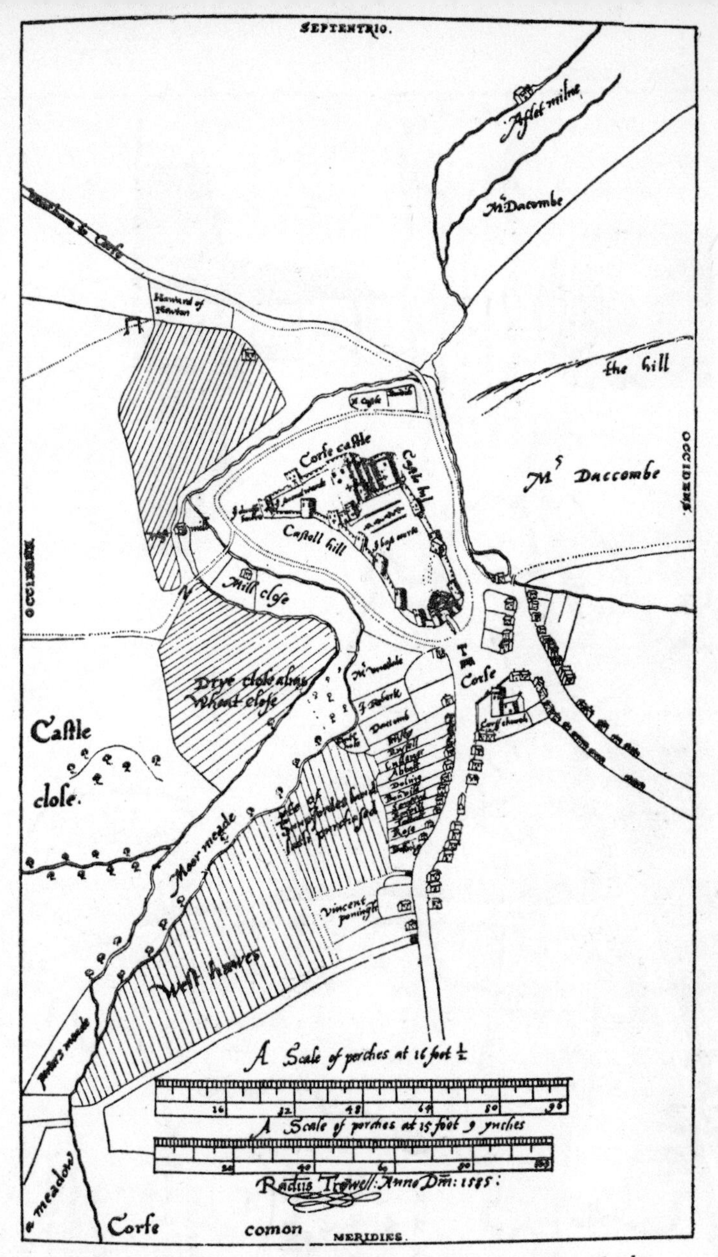

Lithographic Facsimile from Treswell's Plan of the Town and Castle of Corfe. Surveyed in 1585 and Preserved at Kingston Lacy.

Fig 7 Plan of the town and castle of Corfe in 1585 (The plan illustrates very clearly how the little town was totally dominated by the great castle. Although Corfe was a borough and returned two members to Parliament, had a market, and was a centre of the Purbeck stone trade, it remained extremely small, and, like many of the other boroughs and market towns of Dorset, it was in most respects little different from a country village)

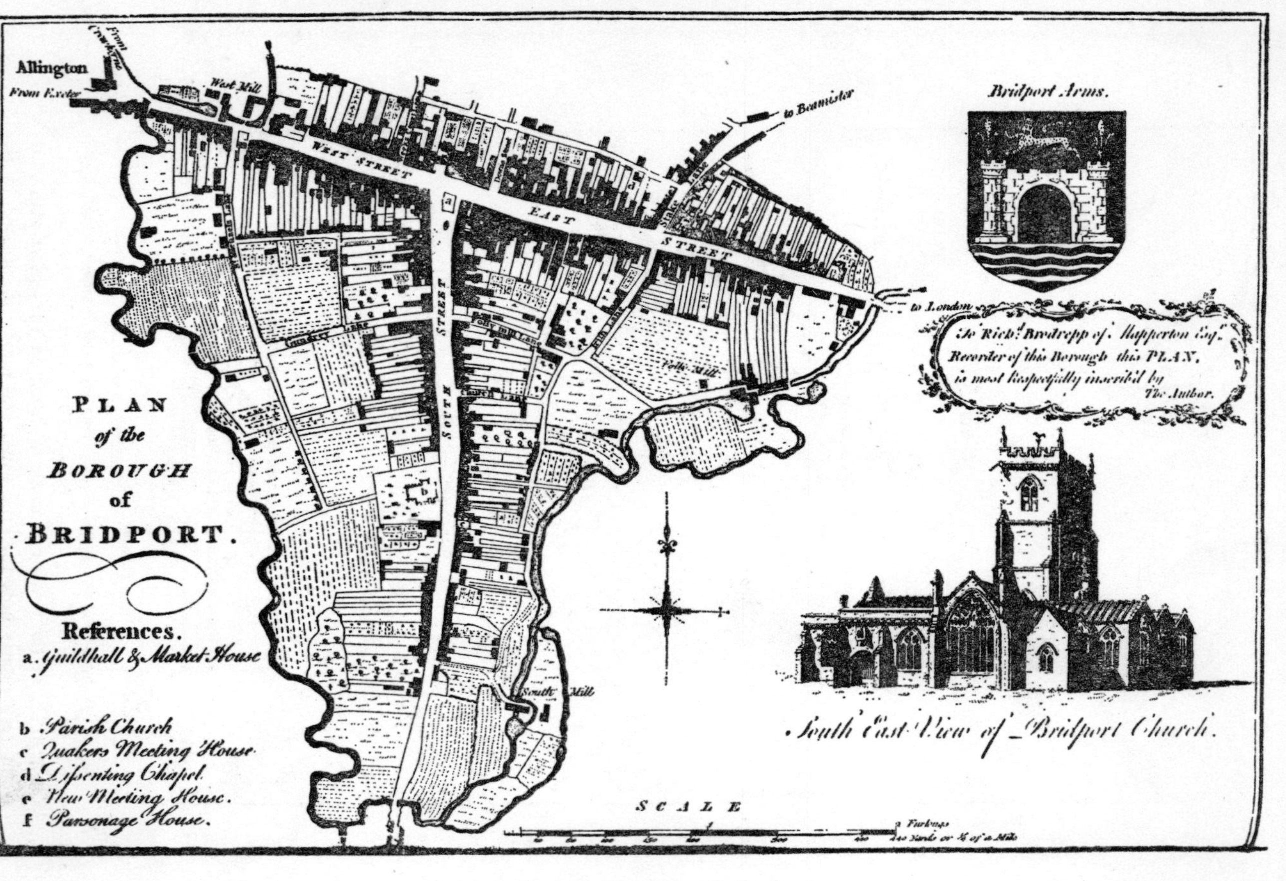

Fig 8 Bridport in the late eighteenth century

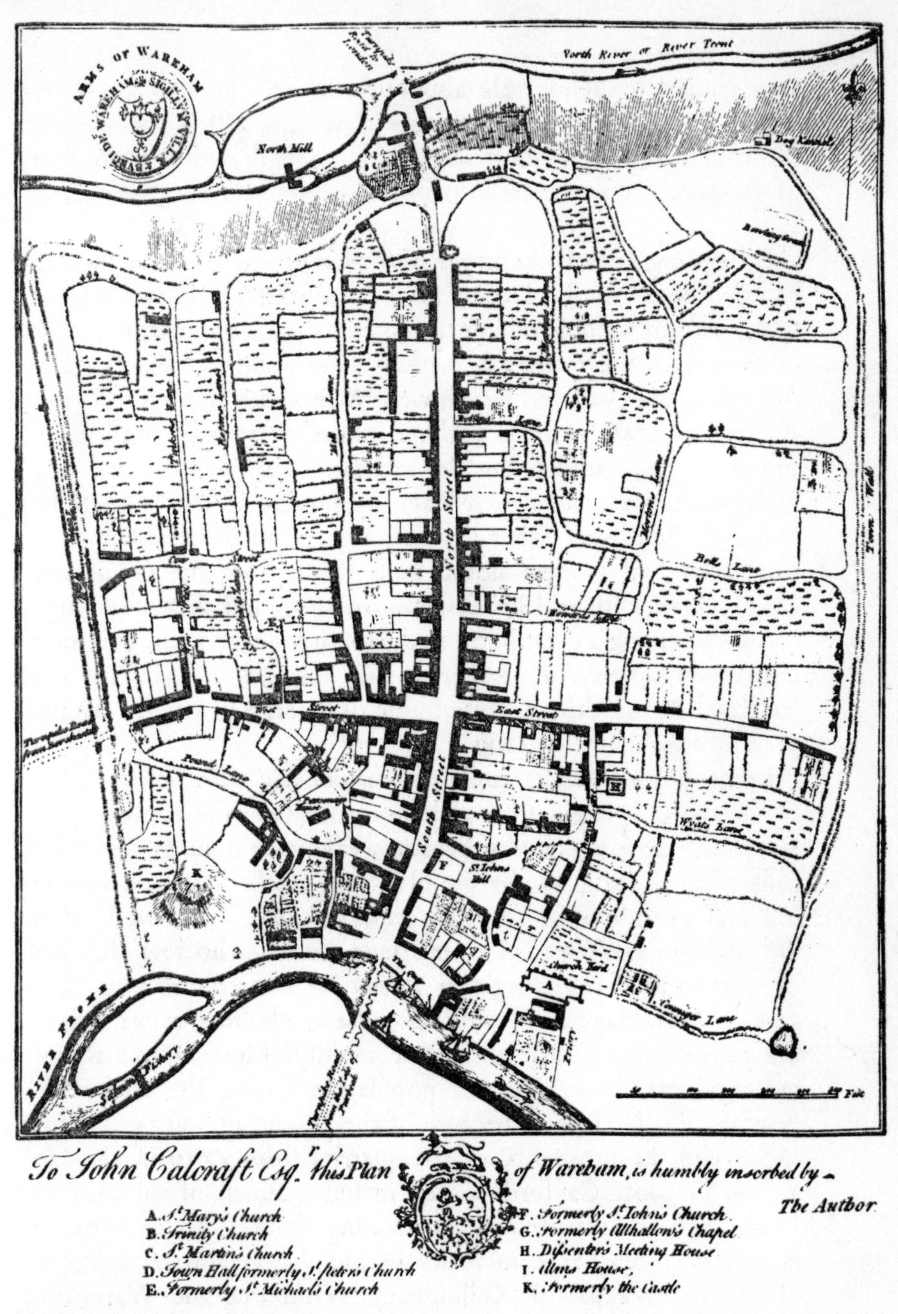

Fig 9 Wareham in the late eighteenth century (The plan shows how easily the whole town was contained within the great Saxon defences, and illustrates how small the towns of Dorset remained until the massive increase in population in the nineteenth and twentieth centuries)

area around his house. He also built the present very attractive village to house his tenants further down the valley out of sight of his mansion. The whole story is the most dramatic illustration of the power possessed by the immensely wealthy landowners of the county.

By the eighteenth century a new phenomenon was beginning to affect some of the Dorset towns, the start of a development which was to become one of the county's most important sources of wealth in the twentieth century—the holiday industry. The first towns to be affected by this were Weymouth and Lyme Regis. As early as 1748 'wooden bathing houses' were erected at Weymouth for sea-bathing, but the real popularity of the town as a resort came with royal patronage, beginning in the 1780s. The Duke of Gloucester spent the winter of 1780 in the town, and soon after had a great house built there, now the Gloucester Hotel. George III paid his first visit in 1789, and thereafter came regularly, giving a great boost to the town as a resort, and bringing it great prosperity, a prosperity still reflected in many of the buildings and in the immense statue of George III erected by the grateful inhabitants in 1809.

Lyme Regis began its career as a fashionable resort even earlier. Defoe stayed there in 1724 and commented enthusiastically upon the society he found, and it became a favourite summer resort for visitors from Bath, as the popularity of sea-bathing and seaside holidays grew during the eighteenth century. The best known visitor from Bath was of course Jane Austen who recorded her impression of Lyme Regis in *Persuasion* written between 1811 and 1816. Swanage also became popular as a holiday resort during the nineteenth century and grew rapidly. Most Dorset towns increased greatly in size and population during the nineteenth century. Portland grew because of the prison, military establishments and the prosperity of the quarries from 1,619 in 1801 to 15,199 in 1901. Canford, which included much of the area of Poole, was equally dramatic increasing from 1,894 in 1801 to 22,069 in 1901. Large increases in population also occurred at Sherborne, Weymouth, Gillingham, Wimborne and Wareham.

A few of the smaller towns declined in the second half of the century, notably Beaminster where the population fell from 2,832 in 1851 to 1,702 in 1901, and Cerne Abbas, which had 1,343 people in 1851, but was down to 643 in 1901. Other places where there was very little growth included Shaftesbury, Bere Regis and Bridport. Some account of the developments during the twentieth century will be given in Chapter 9.

SELECT BIBLIOGRAPHY

M. W. Beresford — *New Towns of the Middle Ages* (1967)

J. Fowler — *Medieval Sherborne* (1951)

D. W. Lloyd — 'Dorchester Buildings' in *Dorset Proceedings*, vol 89 (1958)

J. Newman and N. Pevsner — *The Buildings of England: Dorset* (1952)

R.C.H.M. — *Dorset*

C. C. Taylor — *The Making of the English Landscape: Dorset* (1970)

Victoria County History — *Dorset*, vol II (1908)

M. Weinstock — *Studies in Dorset History* (1953)

More Dorset Studies (1960)

Figures 7, 8 and 9 are taken from J. Hutchins, *The History and Antiquities of Dorset*, 3rd ed (1861–73)

Chapter 5 INDUSTRY AND COMMUNICATIONS

THE Domesday Survey gives little indication of industry, apart from listing 278 mills and various salt pans along the coast. But there were several medieval occupations of importance, including the wool and textile industry, rope and sailcloth, quarrying and fishing. Little is known of the textile industry in the early Middle Ages, but an industry existed if only to serve local needs and to make use of the wool from the large flocks of sheep. The rapid chalk streams of Dorset were used to drive fulling mills for the cloth industry and by the end of the fourteenth century these mills were widely distributed throughout Dorset, and there are references to fulling mills at East Stour, Holt, Wimborne Minster, Kingston Lacy (3 mills), Carey, Rushton, Fordington, Sutton Poyntz (2) and Hooke. Much raw wool was also exported from the county, and a customs house was established at Melcombe in the thirteenth century. In 1364 a staple or official market for wool was set up there. Manufactured cloth was also exported, and in 1376 and 1389 Dorset is mentioned in enactments concerning the evasion of duties and the export of substandard cloth. The county remained, however, on the fringe of the great West of England cloth-producing area. The cloth that was produced compared neither in quality nor quantity with the cloth of Gloucestershire, Somerset or Wiltshire. In 1393 and 1400 Dorset is listed among the counties producing coarse wool and cloth. During the reign of James I a report prepared for the government noted that '. . . the best wolle growen in Devon is better than the dorsetshier wolle by five pence or vj d. in the pound'. It seems likely that any better quality wool and yarn produced was woven into cloth elsewhere. Returns for the number of cloths produced in the South-West counties for c. 1468 are as follows:

Devon	1,036
Dorset	707½
Gloucestershire	1,288
Bristol	3,586½
Somerset	4,981½
Wiltshire	4,310

The principal cloth production of the county by the sixteenth century was 'kersies' and 'Dorset dozens', both coarse woollen fabrics. Many of these cloths were exported to Brittany and Normandy, where they were purchased by poor people 'of a base disposcion' who would not 'go to the price of a good clothe'. Leland commented on the export trade in cloth from Lyme Regis soon after 1535, and noted that 'Merchants of Morleys in Britaine (Morlaix in Brittany) much haunt this town'. He also reported on the cloth industry of Sherborne which 'stondith partely by making of Clothe'.

Some evidence of the wealth derived from the wool and cloth trade in the fifteenth and sixteenth centuries is to be found in the building of so many splendid manor houses and in the enlargement and beautifying of so many of the parish churches of the county during this period.

During the seventeenth century new cloths appeared such as serges and lighter fabrics, while the old kersies continued to be made. Towns engaged in the cloth industry in the seventeenth century included Sherborne, Dorchester, Wareham, Shaftesbury, Sturminster Newton and Gillingham, though most of the actual spinning and weaving was, as always, done as a part-time occupation in labourers' cottages all over the county.

Some account of the industry in the early eighteenth century is given by Defoe in the 1720s. By this time stocking knitting had become an important industry, and at Wimborne he notes that 'the inhabitants who are many, and poor, are chiefly maintained by the manufacture of knitting stockings, which employs a great part indeed of the county of Dorset', and at Stalbridge he records that the whole area was once famous for making 'the finest, best, and highest priz'd knit stockings in England; but that trade is now much decay'd by the encrease of the knitting stocking engine or frame'. Defoe also notes that Poole exported 'all sorts of wearing apparel' and mentions textiles at Dorchester, where serges were made, and at Sherborne.

During the eighteenth century the woollen textile industry in Dorset declined rapidly, though the trade continued to flourish in some places, notably at Shaftesbury and Sturminster where 'swanskin', a coarse white woollen cloth, was made and was used for uniforms and by the Newfoundland fishermen. But by the time of Stevenson's *Survey of the Agriculture of Dorset* in 1812, the trade everywhere was rapidly declining, and never recovered.

As textiles declined, a number of other occupations gained a temporary importance. Among these was the making of buttons, a cottage industry which was very extensive in the eighteenth century, particularly in north Dorset and in which great numbers of women and children were employed. Glove making was also carried on, and large quantities of lace were made in the county at Lyme Regis, Sherborne, Blandford, and elsewhere. Defoe describes the Blandford lace as 'the finest bonelace in England . . . I think I never saw better in Flanders, France or Italy'. Silk manufacture was introduced in the eighteenth century. Its centre was at Sherborne where there is some evidence of the industry in the seventeenth century, but silk spinning was also carried on at Cerne Abbas, Stalbridge, Gillingham and elsewhere. At Sherborne, one of the factory buildings remains and is now used for spinning fibre-glass. And there were, as always in the countryside, a host of other cottage industries.

ROPE AND SAILCLOTH

One of the most important and famous of Dorset industries is the manufacture of ropes, sailcloth, nets, twine, etc which has always been associated with the Bridport area. The rich soils of the Marshwood Vale were highly suitable for growing hemp and flax upon which the industry depended. The earliest firm documentary evidence for the industry comes from the early thirteenth century, when there are accounts for making both rope and nets. In 1213 King John ordered the Sheriff to 'cause to be made at Bridport, night and day, as many ropes for ships both large and small as they could, and twisted yarns for cordage'. There can be little doubt that at this time the industry was already well established. In the early sixteenth century the tight control exercised over the industry in Bridport led to ropewalks being set up in the neighbouring villages, particularly at Burton Bradstock, where the oppressive regulations of Bridport could be avoided. To prevent this happening, the 'Bailiffs, burgesses and other inhabitants of Bridport', secured an Act of Parliament in 1530 which forbade anyone living within five miles of the town from making ropes or from selling hemp except at Bridport market. During the later sixteenth century, therefore, Bridport achieved a virtual monopoly of the trade.

In the seventeenth century Bridport faced foreign competition and also competition from ropewalks established by the Royal Navy at Woolwich, Portsmouth and Plymouth, but Bridport continued to supply great quantities of rope, and in particular supplied the Newfoundland fishing fleets. The fishing industry's main demand was for nets so that ropes became less important. The sailcloth industry also developed rapidly and Bridport took a prominent part in this, though a great deal of sailcloth was manufactured at Beaminster and elsewhere. Stevenson in 1812 commented on the very large numbers of people who were employed in the rope and sailcloth industry, calling it, 'the principal manufactory of this county'.

Dorset was the leading county for the production of both hemp and flax, until the nineteenth century when the acreage devoted to both crops declined dramatically in the face of competition from foreign imports, and the industry became totally dependent on imported raw materials. The industry also received a severe blow during the nineteenth century from the swift decline of the Newfoundland fishery which had previously absorbed so much of its products. It survived by turning to the manufacture of a vast variety of ropes, nets, thread, webbing etc, so that it remains as one of the most important Dorset industries.

During the twentieth century, the industry has been able successfully to change to new materials and man-made fibres, and the various small firms Hounsell, Gundry, Cox and others that had long carried on the trade have amalgamated into the large Bridport Industries Ltd.

THE STONE QUARRYING INDUSTRY

Dorset possesses two stone quarrying areas which have enjoyed national fame and reputation—Purbeck and Portland. The first to be exploited was Purbeck, and the hard stone or marble from cliff top quarries there was used extensively by the Romans, both for tombstones and other memorials, as well as for general architectural purposes. The great period of popularity of Purbeck stone was, however, the thirteenth century, when polished shafts of Purbeck marble became immensely sought-after for church buildings all over England and abroad. The stone was also extensively used during the Middle Ages for effigies, fonts, coffin lids and sepulchral monuments of all kinds. The chief centre of the industry was at Corfe, dominated by the great royal fortress, though the quarries extended over the whole peninsula. It was at Corfe that many of the 'marblers' and quarryowners lived and had their yards for dressing and finishing the stone, for much of it was carved and finished before dispatch. The stone was sent by sea from Ower on the shores of Poole harbour and from several other places along the coast. The demand for Purbeck marble decreased considerably in the later Middle Ages due to changing architectural fashions and to the increasing use of the more easily carved alabaster from Derbyshire and elsewhere, though the Purbeck industry continued to produce carved effigies and tombs up to the sixteenth century and also found a market in supplying the slabs of stone into which the popular brass memorials were fitted.

After the Reformation the demand for the stone for ecclesiastical purposes ceased, but it continued to be quarried for secular buildings, including many of the Dorset manor houses, and roofing tiles and paving slabs were exported from the new port at Swanage. Defoe in the 1720s comments on the use of Purbeck stone in London for 'paving court-yards, alleys, avenues to houses, kitchens, footways on the sides of the highstreets, and the like'. In the nineteenth century the stone was again in demand for church restorations and for the large number of new churches which were being built in the gothic style.

The stone from the Island of Portland does not seem to have been extensively used in the Middle Ages, though some was used locally, and there are isolated references to its use in London, at the Tower and on London Bridge, and at Exeter Cathedral, in the fourteenth century. The amount of stone quarried seems to have been quite small, and it is significant that Leland, who gives a long account of what he saw on Portland, does not mention quarries. It was during the seventeenth century that the really extensive use of Portland stone began. It was used on the Banqueting House at Whitehall and on repairs to old St Paul's before the Fire. After the Fire of 1666 the stone was chosen by Wren for the new St Paul's and for many of the new City churches, and it gained enormous popularity. The demand continued throughout the eighteenth and nineteenth centuries and stone was exported by sea to a great many towns in the British Isles and was also used on the Continent and in America. By the early nineteenth century it was estimated that more than 25,000 tons of stone were being exported annually from the quarries. During the nineteenth century great quantities of Portland stone were also used at the Royal Dockyards at Chatham, Portsmouth and Devonport, as well as being used by convict labour on the Island to construct the massive breakwater and harbour for naval shipping there. In the twentieth century new building techniques have led to a considerably reduced demand for stone, though quarrying continues on the Island. Stone was also quarried elsewhere in Dorset, notably at Sturminster Newton, Marnhull and Long Burton, and at Upwey and Preston near Weymouth. The industry has been, after agriculture, one of the most important employers of labour in the county. At times, notably in the thirteenth and nineteenth centuries, the quarrying, finishing and shipping of stone from the county was by far its most important industrial activity.

FISHING

Fishing has always been an important occupation along the Dorset coast. The Domesday Survey mentions fishermen at Lyme Regis and at Brige (Bridge) in the neighbourhood of Weymouth, and many men no doubt combined fishing with farming or some other occupation and are not therefore listed as fishermen. In 1340 fishing is recorded as important at Portland, Wyke, Weymouth, Preston, Corfe, Studland, Worth, Swanage and Wareham and tithes of fish are also mentioned for many coastal parishes during the Middle Ages. Later medieval records mention herrings, hake, pilchards, ling, mackerel and other fish brought into Dorset harbours, as well as salt fish coming from Brittany, Normandy and elsewhere, often no doubt in return for wool and cloth. A survey of harbours made in Elizabeth's reign lays stress on the importance of fishing in the Dorset ports, and Celia Fiennes who travelled through Dorset in the late seventeenth century also comments on the excellence of the fish to be obtained. For example on the Isle of Purbeck she wrote, 'This is a noted place for lobsters and crabs and shrimps, there I ate some very good.' Poole also had important oyster beds and Defoe described them as 'the best and biggest oysters in all this part of England . . . they are barrell'd up here and sent not only to London but to the West Indies, and to Spain and Italy and other parts'.

By far the most lucrative aspect of the Dorset fishing industry has been the Newfoundland trade in which all the larger ports of Dorset participated, but which was dominated by Poole. Dorset men began fishing off the coasts of Newfoundland in the reign of Elizabeth, and by the reign of James I the trade was already important.

The sole object of the early voyages was fish but the ships soon began to carry ropes, nets and cordage from Bridport, cloth and other articles for trade, and as well as bringing back fish they brought also skins, furs etc. Much of the fish was carried to Spain, Portugal and Italy, though some was sold in England over a very wide area. John Aubrey, the historian of Wiltshire, writing in the latter half of the seventeenth century, wrote of Devizes that it had 'the best market for fish . . . they bring fish from Poole hither, which is sent hence to Oxford'. The Newfoundland trade was immensely important for Dorset and continued until the nineteenth century. It brought great wealth to the merchants engaged in it and was the foundation of the prosperity of Poole. The trade also fostered the shipbuilding and fitting industry as well as providing a very valuable market for home-produced goods.

Other Dorset industries include clay, brewing, pottery, brick-making and a host of minor crafts. Dorset clay from around Poole harbour and Wareham was used by the Romans and continued to be worked during the Middle Ages. Later there was a considerable export trade from Poole in clay for tobacco pipes and pottery. Hutchins, writing in 1773, says that 'Nearly 10,000 tons are exported annually to London, Hull, Liverpool and Glasgow etc, but the most considerable part to Liverpool for the supply of the Staffordshire potteries and to Selby for the use of the Leeds potteries.' Dorset clay is still extracted and continues to be a factor in the economic life of the county.

During the seventeenth and eighteenth centuries several Dorset towns became important malting and brewing centres. Dorchester, Blandford, Shaftesbury and Cerne Abbas were particularly famous for their beer. Thomas Cox in an account of Dorchester written in 1716 remarks that 'since by the French Wars the coming of French Wines is prohibited, the People here have learned to Brew the finest Malt-Liquors in the Kingdom, so delicately clean and well-tasted that the best Judges not only prefer it to the Ales most in vogue, as Hull, Derby, Burton, etc., because 'tis not so heady, but look upon it to be little inferior to common Wine'. The trade declined in the nineteenth century because of competition from places which, having secured early railway links, could transport their produce much more easily and cheaply than the Dorset towns, though brewing continued to supply local needs.

COMMUNICATIONS

The history of the roads of Dorset has been described with a wealth of detail in R. Good's *The Old Roads of Dorset.* Professor Good makes the important point that throughout much of its post-Roman history Dorset was almost entirely avoided by the major through-routes from London to Devon and Cornwall, and that this fact has had important consequences for the history and character of the county. An important feature of the roads of Dorset is the great number and complexity of the ancient trackways in the county; the total length of ancient highways, not counting minor trackways, is 458 miles, of which 380 miles still exist as modern roads or lanes. Two of these ancient trackways stand out as of supreme importance in Dorset. The first is part of a road running from Salisbury to the South West. This trackway enters the corner of the county at a point between Ashmore and Melbury Abbas and is still traceable for much of the fifty miles across Dorset to Lambert's Castle, a hillfort just across the Devon border. It was obviously of much more than local importance, and probably formed a vital link in the communication network of prehistoric southern England.

The second is the Southern Ridgeway which is still very evident for much of its length across the southern part of the county, and which possibly ran originally the whole distance from the Isle of Purbeck to the Devon border and beyond. This Ridgeway is marked along the whole of its length by burial sites and mounds, a fact which may suggest that it was already in use at an early date. Few roads can have such a dense concentration of barrows along their length, and few can equal the views from it across the Chesil Beach to Portland and the English Channel. These two trackways are only among the more important of a vast and complicated pattern of prehistoric routes which covered much of the county. They provided an elaborate system of communications which existed long before the coming of the Romans, and much of which continued to be used by pack-horse traffic and for cattle-droving until the coming of the railways.

The Romans added a comparatively small mileage to these ancient trackways, and often used the route of a trackway for their own roads, as, for example, between Dorchester and Eggardon. The new roads which were built by the Romans enabled rapid troop movements to be made, and were themselves part of the process of conquest. The sheer size, width and technical excellence of the new roads and the employment of vast numbers of native labourers in their construction must have brought home very forcibly to the populace that they now had new and fiercely energetic masters. In Dorset the basic road system created by the Romans was very simple. The principal road was the great through-route from London to Exeter by way of Silchester, Salisbury, Badbury and Dorchester. This entered Dorset near Woodyates and is still clearly to be seen on the ground. Some of the northern parts of this road are among the best and most impressive surviving stretches of Roman road in Britain.

A second Roman road ran from Poole harbour northward to Badbury and thence on into Wiltshire. The third road ran from Weymouth northwards through Dorchester to Yeovil and on to the Fosse Way at Ilchester. This road is still for much of its length the modern highway.

After the Romans there was little new road building until the coming of the turnpikes in the eighteenth century. But a great many new trackways came into existence during the late Saxon and early medieval periods. The roads of west Dorset, of the Marshwood Vale and the Blackmoor Vale, with their tortuous windings and apparently pointless sudden turns show very clearly their origin in a period of the expansion of settlement into forest and woodland waste. A good example is the attractive winding road from Whitchurch Canonicorum to Stoke Abbott, which meanders through the Vale linking a number of undoubtedly ancient farmsteads. Many similar examples are to be found elsewhere in the county.

Defoe early in the eighteenth century encountered a difficulty which must have beset travellers across the downs of Dorset and Wiltshire for many centuries: 'Shaftesbury is fourteen miles from Salisbury over that fine down or carpet ground, which they call particularly, or properly, Salisbury Plain. It has neither house or town in view all the way, and the road which often lyes very broad, and branches off insensibly, might easily cause a traveller to loose his way.'

We are reminded that the roads were generally without sign-posts, and that since they were inadequately surfaced they tended to become very wide as successive travellers sought routes free from mud and potholes. Defoe found his way because 'there is a certain never failing assistance upon all these downs for telling a stranger his way, and that is the number of shepherds feeding, or keeping their vast flocks of sheep, which are every where in the way, and who, with a very little pains, a traveller may always speak with . . .'

The roads of Dorset, as elsewhere, were revolutionised by the coming of the turnpikes during the eighteenth century. The turnpike roads of Dorset fell under no less than twenty-five trusts, nearly all of which were set up between 1750 and 1780. All had ceased to operate by 1883. At the height of their popularity and influence, about 1840, before the railway came, the turnpike trusts of Dorset comprised about 500 miles of road. Professor Good sums up the effect of the turnpikes in the county as follows:

> The effects of the turnpike trusts on local road communication was profound. Until they came the road system was one which had grown up, almost casually over many centuries, and which could not therefore be expected to mould itself quickly to changing circumstances. On this old pattern the turnpikes impressed a new outline, designed more to meet the requirements of the times . . . so it is today, that though there are many main roads that were never turnpikes, there is scarcely an old turnpike which is not still an important traffic artery and likely long to remain so.

But the turnpikes with their carrier services, coaches and waggons affected only a small part of the county and a very small proportion of the roads. Many places remained throughout the nineteenth century very isolated.

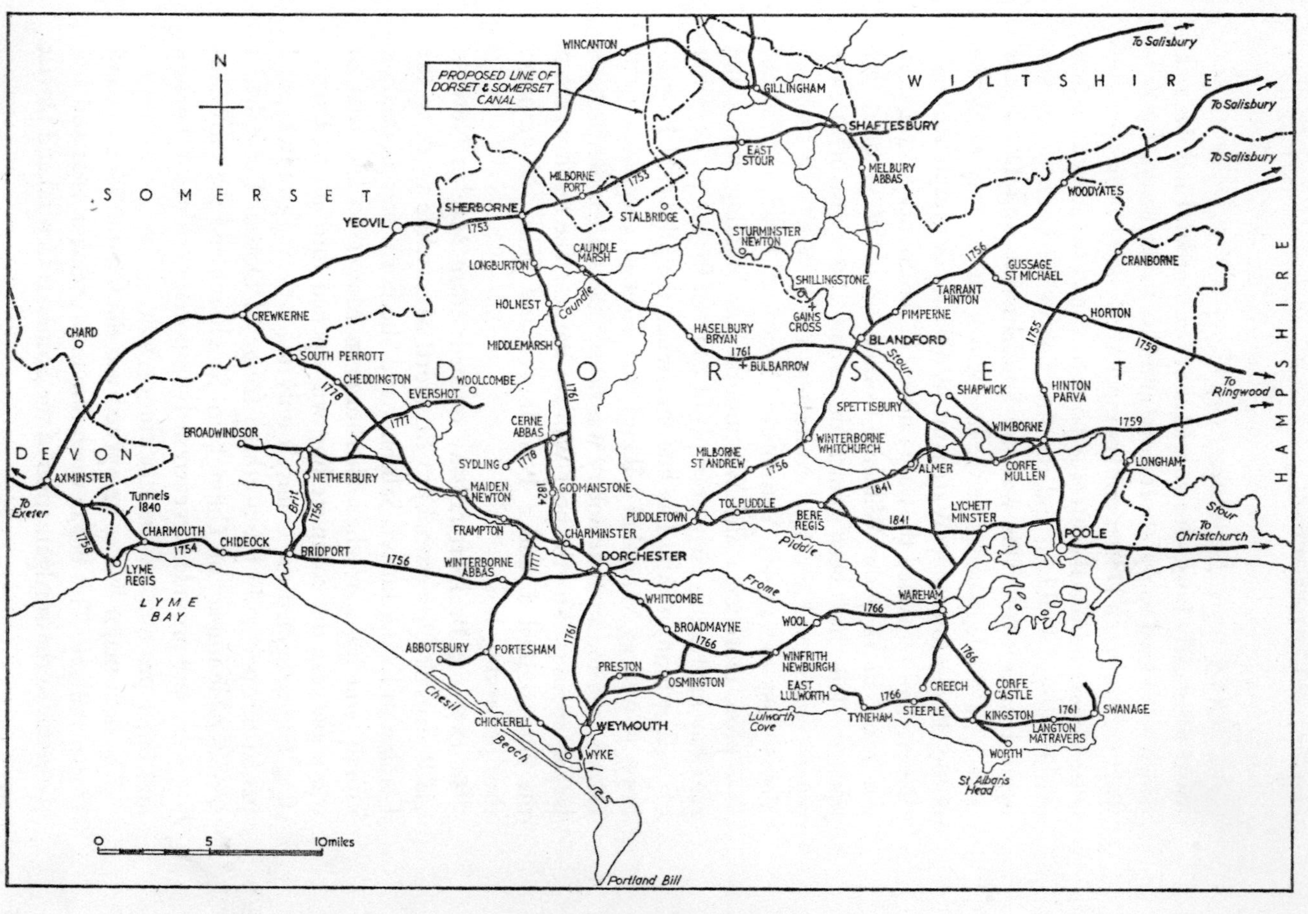

Fig 10 Turnpike roads

RAILWAYS

Apart from early horse-drawn tramways on Portland and Purbeck which were used to transport stone and clay to the quays, the railways did not reach Dorset until comparatively late. There were no large towns, industrial centres or ports to attract the early attention of the railway builders, and the first line in the county was not opened until 1847. This was the Southampton and Dorchester railway, a single, narrow-gauge line which ran by way of Wimborne, Poole Junction, Wareham, Wool and Moreton to Dorchester. This remained the only railway in the county for the next ten years. In 1857 the Wiltshire Somerset and Weymouth line opened. This had been under discussion and construction for several years, and the final route was from Westbury through Yeovil and thence via Yetminster, Evershot, Maiden Newton, Frampton, Dorchester and Weymouth. The building of this line raised an interesting early example of concern for the preservation of ancient monuments. The line threatened the hillfort at Poundbury as well as Maumbury Rings, the Roman amphitheatre in Dorchester, and a public outcry was raised against their destruction, largely sponsored by the poet William Barnes. The result was that the line tunnelled under Poundbury, and skirts Maumbury, thus preserving both.

In 1857 the Bridport railway opened; from Maiden Newton via Poorstock (Powerstock) to Bridport. Meanwhile work on the London to Exeter line via Salisbury and Sherborne was proceeding rapidly and trains reached Sherborne in May 1860 and later in the same year the complete line was opened through to Exeter. This line remained the county's only main through railway, and passed through only the northern fringe of Dorset. But it had a considerable impact on Gillingham, Sherborne and the surrounding areas, and provided an extremely important outlet for the milk and other products of the Blackmoor Vale.

The next major line to be opened was the famous Somerset and Dorset railway. This began operating in September 1862 and was the result of the amalgamation of the Somerset Central and Dorset

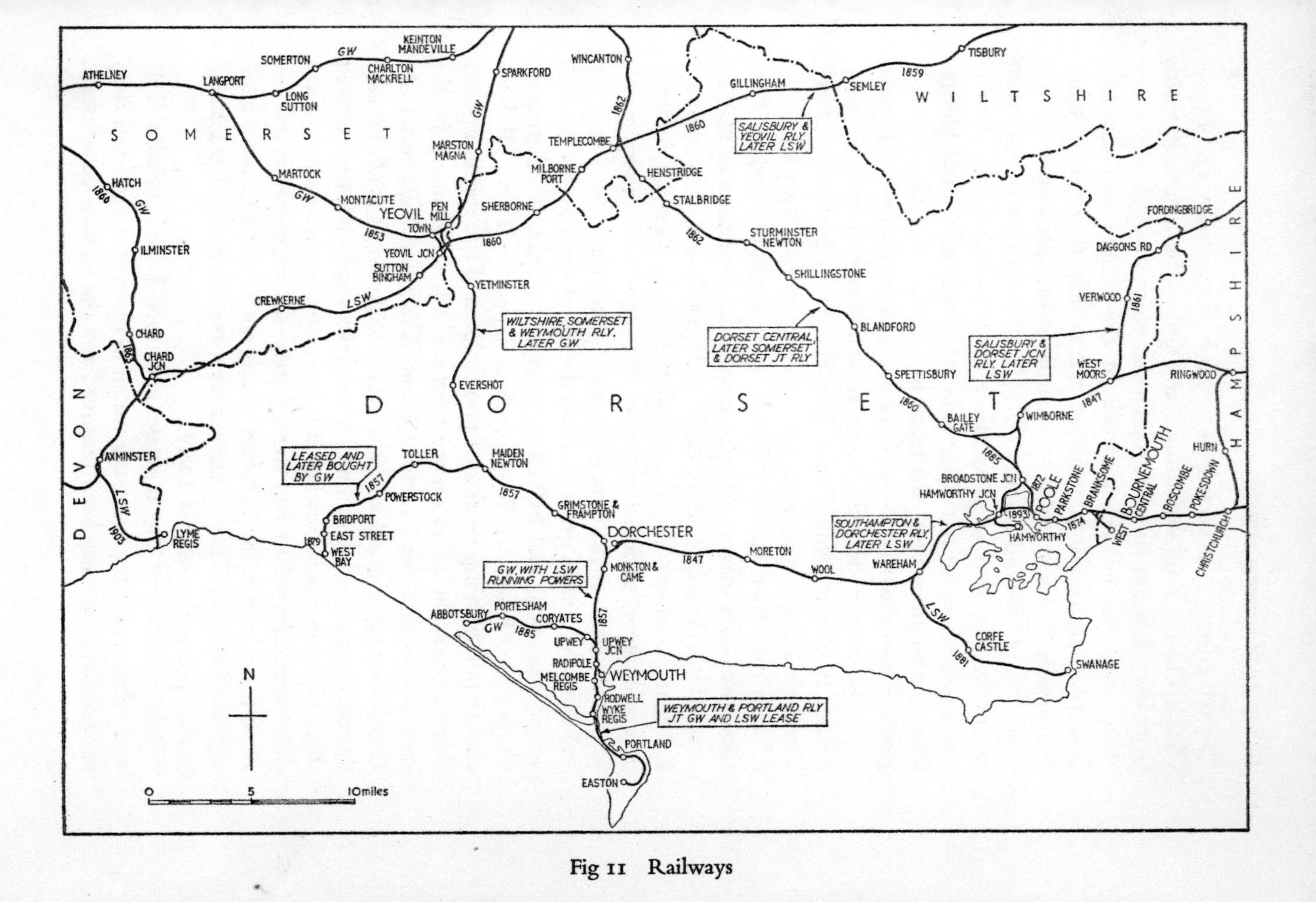

Fig 11 Railways

Central railways. It served as a direct route from the Bristol Channel to the English Channel, and also enabled through trains from the Midlands to reach the Dorset coast.

By 1885 the railway network of the county was virtually finished, a tremendous achievement in less than forty years. The system was completed by the time of the agricultural depression of the 1880s and 90s and the railways provided an important means for labourers to escape from the county and seek work in more prosperous areas and abroad. Social ties and the old tightly-knit communities were shattered by this impact. The marriage registers also show how the railways, and no doubt the bicycle, led to marriages between partners who lived in villages much farther apart than would have been the case a few years before. The railways also provided a number of reasonably paid secure jobs, an important fact in a time of agricultural depression. They also provided a gleam of hope through the depression in making it possible to transport milk easily and quickly out of the county. For arable farmers also the railways brought new implements, drainage pipes, artificial manures etc, and made possible the implementation of many new ideas and methods.

The railway had a great effect on the life of those towns through which it passed, and helped to change for example Sherborne, Gillingham, Bridport, Weymouth and perhaps above all Dorchester into bustling centres of population and enterprise. Equally dramatic was the effect on the towns which were missed by the railways, so that, for example, Cerne Abbas and Beaminster declined very rapidly and virtually ceased to be towns at all. Equally dramatic was the effect on the turnpike roads where a serious slump in traffic and consequently in income occurred, and where the coaches ceased to run immediately the railways opened. In 1855, for example, the last stage coach ran through Cerne Abbas, and the town, avoided by the railway, was thereafter left isolated and its prosperity melted away.

Today many of the railways constructed so hopefully little more than a century ago, have ceased to operate and in some cases the lines have already been removed and the stations demolished.

Now the only access to most of the towns and villages of Dorset is once again by road.

SELECT BIBLIOGRAPHY

J. H. Bettey — *The Island and Royal Manor of Portland* (1970)
'The Supply of Stone for Re-building St Paul's Cathedral' (*Archaeological Journal*, vol 128, 1972)

D. G. Drury — 'The Use of Purbeck Marble in Medieval Times' (*Dorset Proceedings*, vol 70, 1948)

R. Good — *The Old Roads of Dorset* (1966)

G. B. Grundy — 'The Ancient Highways of Dorset etc' (*Archaeological Journal*, vol 94, 1937)

J. H. Lucking — *Railways of Dorset* (1968)

Victoria County History — *Dorset*, vol II (1908)

F. C. Warren — 'Dorset Industries of the Past' (*Dorset Proceedings*, vol 59, 1937)

M. B. Weinstock — *Old Dorset* (1967)

Chapter 6 THE CHURCH

THE most remarkable feature of the religious scene in medieval Dorset was the great number of its ancient religious houses and their size. About these a good deal is known and has been written, whereas very little work has been done on the parish life of Dorset during the Middle Ages, and comparatively little can be said with certainty concerning the parish churches, their services, the life and thoughts of the clergy or the spiritual ideals and aspirations of the people. It is necessary to keep this in mind when looking at the medieval church in Dorset in order to avoid gaining an unbalanced impression, and giving too great a prominence to the monastic houses.

A major result of the Norman Conquest was that the see of Sherborne was transferred to Old Sarum, and subsequently, during the early thirteenth century, to Salisbury. Dorset became an archdeaconry of the diocese of Salisbury, and remained so until 1542, when it was transferred to the newly created and oddly constituted bishopric of Bristol, which consisted of Bristol and some neighbouring parishes together with Dorset, and had as its cathedral the church of the former Augustinian abbey in Bristol. This curious situation lasted until 1836 when Dorset was once again made part of the diocese of Salisbury.

The Domesday Survey shows clearly the very strong territorial position of the church in the county. More than a third of the land was in ecclesiastical possession, and the Church lands were greater in extent than the combined possessions of all the great barons and important landholders. The bishop of Salisbury held no less than sixteen manors, besides various lands and properties in the boroughs and other places and was, after the king, the wealthiest man in the county, while eleven abbots and four abbesses also held lands. Amongst these were the heads of the great ancient monastery of Sherborne, the largest of the Dorset monasteries, the nunnery of Shaftesbury, the largest and richest in all England, and the monastic houses of Cerne, Milton, Abbotsbury, Cranborne and Horton as well as a number of houses outside Dorset.

The Domesday Book does not set out to give information about parish churches, but a few churches are included incidentally. Churches are mentioned at Burton Bradstock, Bridport, Whitchurch Canonicorum, Wareham where there were two churches, at Bere Regis, Dorchester, Gillingham, Winfrith Newburgh, Puddletown, Chaldon and Fleet and a chapel at Wimborne Minster. Clearly these were not all the parish churches in Dorset at that time. It is apparent from architectural evidence, for example, that there were Saxon churches at Sherborne and elsewhere, and there were early minster churches at Yetminster, Charminster, Beaminster, Iwerne Minster and Sturminster, which are not mentioned. It is impossible to tell from the Domesday Survey how far the parochial organisation of the county had proceeded by that time. It is probable, however, that, as in neighbouring counties, the division of Dorset into definite parishes each with its parish church was completed soon after the end of the twelfth century, though we have no certain knowledge of this interesting and important development.

The twelfth and thirteenth centuries saw the addition to the old Benedictine monasteries of a number of houses of the new reformed orders, as well as the establishment of several colleges, hospitals, almshouses, etc. A reformed Benedictine or Cluniac priory was established at East Holme about 1150 as a dependent cell of Montacute in Somerset, and before the end of the twelfth century the Cistercian order had founded an abbey at Bindon and a nunnery at Tarrant Crawford. This nunnery was to become particularly well known and favoured, and it was for the nuns at Tarrant Crawford that the great Bishop Richard Poore of Salisbury, bishop there from 1217 to 1229, compiled the Ancren

Riwle or Rule for Anchoresses, with its eminently sensible advice to the nuns on their life and conduct and its warm human touches, warning the sisters not to be too severe upon themselves, recognising that there were difficulties to be overcome, such as the insolence of 'Slurry the cook's boy who washes dishes in the kitchen', and containing the homely injunction, 'Ye shall not possess any beast, my dear sisters, except only a cat.'

Several smaller houses were also established. For example, the Knights Hospitallers at Friar Mayne, the Dominican friars at Gillingham and Melcombe Regis, the Franciscans at Dorchester, and a number of other establishments including several short-lived alien priories. Details of all these religious houses and hospitals are given in the *Victoria County History: Dorset*, vol II (1908). Forde Abbey, the site of which is now in Dorset, was throughout the Middle Ages part of Devon.

Of the great monastic buildings only a very small proportion survive. The magnificent churches at Sherborne and Milton provide some indication of the former splendour of the monasteries. So too does the barn at Abbotsbury, or the Abbot's Hall porch at Cerne, almost all that remains there of the great abbey buildings which once dominated the lovely valley, presided over by the brooding pagan presence of the Cerne Giant. Perhaps the almshouse at Sherborne best preserves the spirit and atmosphere of medieval religious life. The main structure of the building, dating from the 1440s, survives as planned with its lovely chapel intact, and the building continues to fulfil its original function as an almshouse.

Little survives of the works of art or the libraries of the monastic houses. Perhaps the best example to survive is the Sherborne Missal and a Lectionary, the script of which was written by John Whas, a monk of Sherborne, and which was illuminated by John Sifrewas a Dominican friar. Both books were probably produced in the abbey at Sherborne. The superb illumination of the Missal contains miniature portraits of the bishop of Salisbury, the abbot of Sherborne, Whas and Sifrewas themselves, as well as a wealth of scriptural and devotional material and a series of common

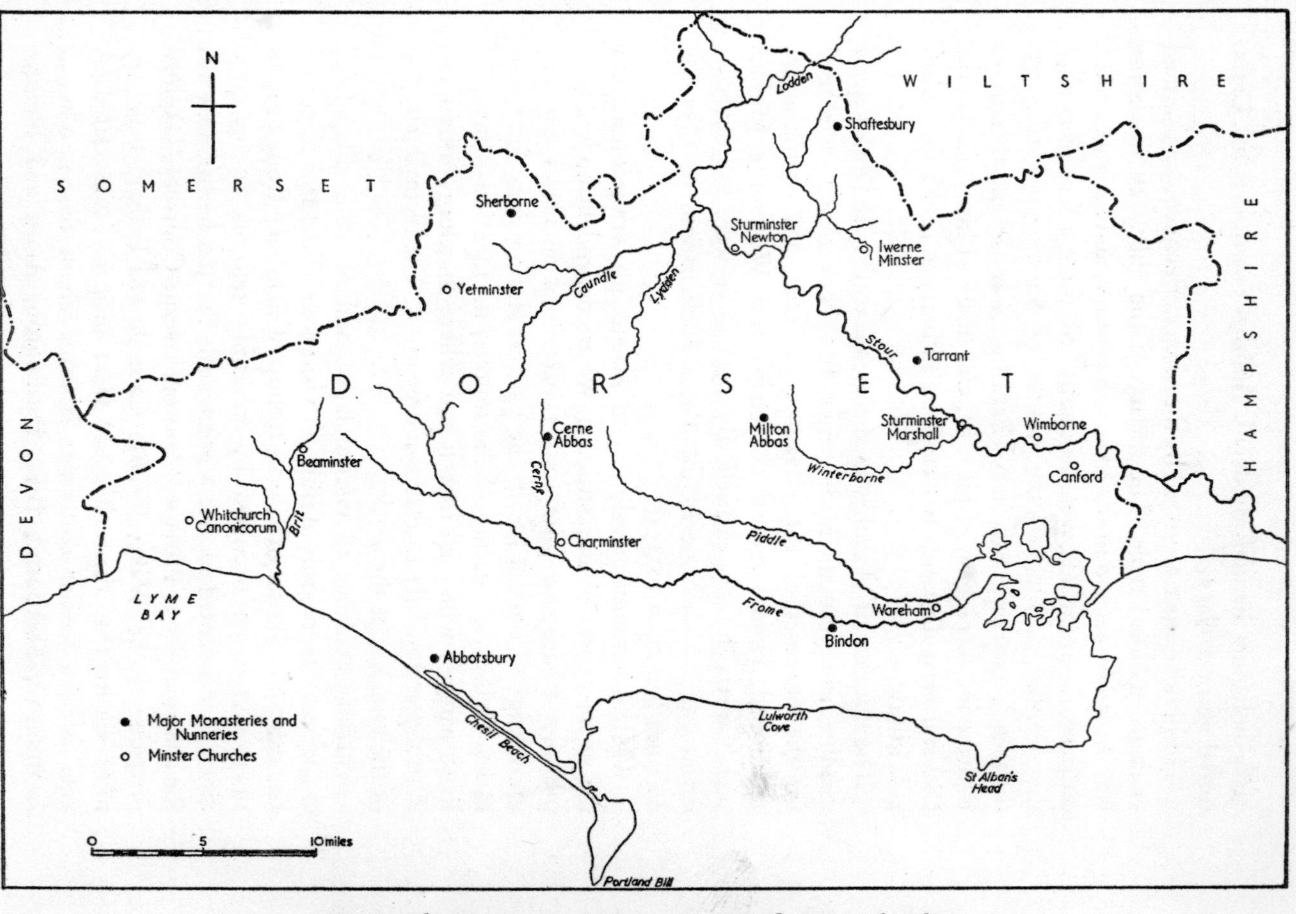

Fig 12 The major monasteries, nunneries and minster churches

birds and other naturalistic detail. Another example is the Cerne missal and cartulary.

The libraries once possessed by the monasteries have also vanished virtually without trace. The library of the abbey at Sherborne was visited by Leland in the sixteenth century, and he commented on the volumes which were evidently still there a few years after the dissolution. One of the monks of Sherborne during the thirteenth century, Adam of Barking, was the most famous Benedictine theologian of his time, and many of his works on the Old and New Testaments were in the library at Sherborne when Leland saw it.

The number of churches in the archdeaconry of Dorset grew steadily throughout the Middle Ages. In a list of churches compiled for the purposes of Papal taxation in 1291, 171 churches are mentioned, besides several chapelries, and Wimborne Minster which was a deanery in itself. By 1341 there were 218 churches listed, and by the time of the Valor Ecclesiasticus in 1535 the number had risen to 234.

Whilst it is comparatively easy to trace the growth and functioning of the church as an institution, we are dependent upon a few, pitifully inadequate glimpses of occasional incidents for our knowledge of church life in the parishes during these long centuries. In the very nature of the sources, no mention is made of those parishes where all is well and where the clergy ministered dutifully and quietly to their congregations. The records tell only of the criminal or the weak.

There is evidence of clerical lapses and of some dilapidated churches in the records of bishop's visitations of the archdeaconry. For example, Simon of Ghent, bishop of Salisbury from 1297 to 1315, was much occupied by imposing reforms on his large diocese, and visited Dorset a great deal. In 1302 he had to warn the clergy of Stour Provost, Manston, Iwerne Courtney, Okeford Fitzpaine, Stoke Wake, Bishops Caundle and Pulham that they must ensure that their churches were properly consecrated. A year later, a similar complaint is made about the churches at Beaminster, Sherborne, Bere, Fordington, Alton and Netherbury—all churches appropriated to prebends in Salisbury Cathedral —which are said to be 'destitute of consecration'. At Shaftesbury in 1311 the bishop ordered that the rough games in the churchyard should stop, and that animals should not be allowed to graze among the graves. Pluralist and nonresident clergy are also noted in various parts of the county and successive bishops made efforts to stamp out this abuse but with little success. Simon of Ghent's register shows the bishop also concerned with a host of minor human failings and difficulties of the clergy—failure to provide all the services, unreasonable extortions by the prebendary at Yetminster, missing books, ornaments or vessels necessary for divine service, etc. The rector of Winterborne Stickland who was a foreigner was enjoined to find a chaplain to teach him the English language.

But the very fact that churches were in need of consecration is in itself evidence of popular piety and concern for enlarging, rebuilding and beautifying the church buildings. In 1326 Robert Petyt a suffragan bishop consecrated or reconsecrated no less than forty-six churches in Dorset after building work. The fact, too, that so many clergy perished in the plagues of the fourteenth century, as mentioned in Chapter 3, is some indication that they were in their parishes and in contact with the sick and dying during the onslaughts of the epidemic. The few surviving late medieval churchwardens' accounts, for example of All Hallows, Sherborne and of Wimborne Minster, also give a splendid picture of vigorous religious life in these communities. And the dispute between the parishioners of All Hallows, Sherborne and the monks of the adjoining abbey in the 1430s which led to the great fire in the abbey church, whilst providing evidence of the violence and brutality of medieval life, is also proof of the vital concern of the parishioners over their church and their intense desire to use it without interruption. During the fifteenth century almost every church in Dorset was rebuilt, enlarged or beautified in some way or, most noticeably, had a tower added.

The workmanship and splendour of the churches of, for example, Cerne Abbas, Bere Regis, Yetminster, Wyke Regis,

Buckland Newton, Puddletown and a host of others, or the superb towers of Beaminster, Piddletrenthide, Bradford Abbas, St Peter's in Dorchester and many others, provide magnificent witness to the strength of late medieval piety, as well as to the prosperity of the times, which made all this building activity possible.

THE REFORMATION

Only one monastery in the county had an annual income of less than £200 and so came under the provisions of the Act for the Dissolution of the Smaller Monasteries of 1536. This was the Cistercian house of Bindon which according to the Valor Ecclesiasticus was worth £147 7 9¾ per annum. The monastery managed to avoid being dissolved under the terms of the 1536 Act by a payment to the king of £300, though it gained only a very temporary respite by this manoeuvre, and was finally brought to an end, together with all the other Dorset monasteries in 1539. The example of Bindon probably encouraged other monasteries to hope that they might also prolong their existence by similar means, and in 1538 both the abbess of Shaftesbury and the abbot of Cerne offered sums of money to the king and to Thomas Cromwell in order to be allowed to continue. These offers were of no avail, and in little more than a week during March 1539, all the great Dorset monasteries were swept away. The King's Commissioners, Dr William Petre and Dr John Tregonwell, having dissolved Forde Abbey, just across the border in Devon on 8 March 1539 received the surrender of Milton on 11 March, Abbotsbury on the 12th, Tarrant Crawford on the 13th, Bindon on the 14th, Sherborne and its cell at Horton on the 18th, East Holme on the 20th, and Shaftesbury on the 23rd. The Priory of Cranborne was a dependency of Tewkesbury and survived until January 1540. In 1547 the chantries, colleges, hospitals were likewise suppressed and further stores of wealth passed into the king's hands.

After the dissolution of the monasteries and chantries, the next most obvious signs of change came during the reign of Edward VI, and in the parish churches—the introduction of the English services in 1549, the taking down of the images and the great rood screen with its figures, the obliteration or destruction of so many wall paintings, stained glass windows and other 'relics of popery', and the confiscation by the King's Commissioners of all the surplus plate and other valuables of the churches. No parish could retain more than the bare minimum required for the celebration of the services, and always the worst or least valuable plate was left and the more valuable confiscated. One example must serve as an illustration of what happened in all the churches, of the splendour and magnificence of the church goods which were confiscated:

Gillingham: Inventory of Church Goods 1552

First i crose of sylver parcel gylt
i Senser of syler (Censer of silver)
i shippe of sylver (for carrying the incense)
i paxe of sylver (pax for the Kiss of peace)
ii cruetes of sylver (cruets)
ii chalecis of sylver and gylt (chalices)
i cope of Red valvet
i wlyt cope of sylke,
i of blacke saye
i of red
i of grene
i suyte of red velvet
i purple a nother suyt of whyte
i blewe
i black
i newe vestment of whyt
i blewe vestment of Damask,
i vestment of whyt
i old cheseble
ii clothes of dyaper for the table
ii clothes of holond for the table
ii clothes that dyd hang before the vont (font)
ii towelles for the lavetory
ii surplecis
ii Rochetes
ii peyre of organes,
iii lynen clothes

i crose of brase
i censar of brase
iiii candelstycks of brase
a paxe of brase
i holy water pot of brase
iiii banners of sarcenet
ii streyners
ii curtyns
iii cushines
iii corporas
i oyle vate of Tynne (for the holy oils)
V great belles
i lytele bell

To the Churches use
Apoynted by the said commissioners the chalis, the cope of Crymeson velvet with all the table clothes and surpleses, the rest commytted to the charg of them under wrytten

Thomas Hankines	Curat
John Mathewe	
Thomas Aishe	Churchwardens
Nicholas Rykes	
John Garret	
John Stone	Parishioners
Walter Henbury	

In the midst of these upheavals, in 1542, Dorset was transferred from the diocese of Salisbury to the newly created diocese of Bristol. Such a change of diocese was not easily accepted in a conservative rural area, and as late as 1577 two Deputy Lieutenants, Sir John Horsey and George Trenchard, justified to the Privy Council their difficulty in obtaining information about Catholics on the grounds that 'it was uncertain in whose diocese the shire was'. Those who wish to follow the course of the Reformation in detail in one particular Dorset town, can read the splendidly clear and dramatic account of the changes in Sherborne in Joseph Fowler's book *Medieval Sherborne*. Particularly full documentary and architectural evidence survives concerning the course and effect of the Reformation changes in Sherborne. The vicar, John Chetmill, remained in his post throughout all the changes from the reign of Henry VIII to that of Elizabeth, and saw the monks go from the abbey, the Bible and services in English introduced, the confiscations and alterations in his church, All Hallows, and eventually the great abbey church become his own parish church. It would all have seemed very improbable to him when he first became vicar in 1539.

All the manifold changes of the sixteenth century, including the remarkable but short-lived reversal of the general trend during the reign of Mary, and the return to Protestantism under Elizabeth seem to have provoked no protest in Dorset. The dissolution of the great Dorset monasteries produced no violent reaction even in places such as Abbotsbury, Cerne, Sherborne or Wimborne where the whole life of the place was bound up with the religious houses and institutions. Later, in 1549 there was no response in Dorset to the attempts made by the men of Cornwall and Devon to cling on to the old ways and to oppose the new church services. A number of Dorset families emerged as stoutly Catholic during the reign of Elizabeth, but many of them had not stood firm earlier, but like the Stourtons, the Tregonwells, the Turbervilles, or even the Arundels, and, like a great many other Catholic families elsewhere who were later to be so loyal to the old faith, they had profited greatly from the sales of monastic lands and other perquisites of the Reformation.

Catholicism continued to have a good deal of support in Dorset. Most people found it impossible to remain loyal to the old religion in the face of strenuous governmental pressure, but nonetheless some of the oldest families in the county remained stubbornly Catholic during the reign of Elizabeth, including the Turbervilles of Bere Regis, the Martyns of Athelhampton, the Stourtons of Canford and, ironically, some of the Tregonwells of Milton Abbey whose fortunes were very firmly founded upon the ruin of the monasteries. Most notable of all were the Arundels of Chideock near Bridport, who were able to encourage and support many Dorset Catholics, and whose house became the chief centre of Catholicism. Most of the Catholic priests executed in the county during the late sixteenth century had been chaplains at Chideock.

The most notable of the priests was Blessed John Cornelius, a Cornishman who had become a Jesuit and returned to England in 1583. He spent eleven years in England at various Arundel houses in Cornwall, Dorset, London and elsewhere, converting, strengthening and encouraging the Catholic laity. In 1594 he was taken at Chideock, and for a time was kept as a prisoner at Sir George Trenchard's house, Wolfeton, where he disputed with many Dorset notables, including Sir Walter Raleigh, and left a very deep impression on many of those who spoke with him. Subsequently he was tried, found guilty of treason, and executed at Dorchester in July 1594. Other Catholics from Dorset executed during Elizabeth's reign included John Mundyn of Mapperton who had been a schoolmaster. He was captured and executed in London in 1584. Another priest, Thomas Pilchard, was executed at Dorchester in 1584, and a layman, William Pike from Parley, a joiner by trade, was executed for his faith at Dorchester in 1591. These are a few of those who, in Dorset as elsewhere, found themselves implicated in a web composed of religion, international diplomacy and fear of foreign invasion or of popular insurrection, and suffered in consequence. Dorset also had the curious distinction during the reign of Elizabeth of producing the man who, perhaps more than any other was responsible for bringing Mary Queen of Scots to the block. This was Arthur Gregory of Lyme Regis who in Fuller's words, 'had the art of forcing the seal of a letter; yet so invisibly, that it still appeared a virgin to the exactest beholder'. He was employed by Walsingham to open the Queen of Scots' letters and thus secure details of the Babington Plot. Later, a large part in the survival of Catholicism in the county was to be played by the Husseys of Marnhull, the Webbs of Canford, and, above all, by the Welds of Lulworth. It was at Lulworth that the first Catholic church to be erected in England since the Reformation was built in 1786–7.

The Catholics remained, however, a minority, and it was Puritanism that was to become the strongest religious force in the county. The town of Poole became the earliest stronghold of Protestantism, due largely to the influence of the zealous and energetic Protestant minister there from the beginning of the reign of Edward VI (1547), Thomas Hancock. Hancock has left a brief fragment of autobiography from which it is possible to gain some idea of the success of his preaching in Poole. Hancock himself says of the people of Poole that 'they were the first thatt in thatt parte of England were called Protestantes'. In the reign of Mary, Hancock was forced to go abroad, or, as he puts it, 'for savegard of my lyfe too flee'. He went first to France and later to Geneva where he became a member of Knox's congregation. His later history is uncertain, but he may have returned to Dorset with the accession of Elizabeth. Another member of Knox's congregation, William Kethe, author of the famous 'Old Hundredth' returned in 1561 to become rector of Child Okeford.

Puritan sentiment grew very rapidly during the late sixteenth and early seventeenth century. By 1634, when Archbishop Laud's representatives carried out his Metropolitan visitation, they complained that there were Puritans in nearly every parish in Dorset. They also reported that in nearly every parish, Puritan churchwardens were chosen and that these frustrated all efforts of the church authorities to carry out Laud's ideas as to the furnishings and services of the church. There is no doubt that a great many of the inhabitants of Dorset in the early seventeenth century would have liked to see the Reformation carried still further, and desired to have the remaining 'relics of Popery' banished from the Church of England. Many would no doubt have agreed with the Minister at Halstock who was reported by the scandalised churchwardens in 1613 for having said in his sermon that 'it were better to eate or drinke before we came to ye communion than to think of our breakfast at home. And that it made no matter whether we received it sitting, standing or kneeling but that in his opinion it might best be done sitting'.

The Puritans were particularly strong in the towns. In Sherborne the zealous Puritan preacher William Lydford, was vicar from 1632 to 1653. Puritan feeling was also strong in Beaminster, where the minister was reported in 1616 for not praying for archbishops and bishops, and where, at the beginning of the Civil War, the townsmen were said to be violently opposed to the king and the church hierarchy. Poole, Weymouth, Lyme Regis and Dorchester were also strongly Puritan. At Dorchester the most powerful influence was John White, the rector of Holy Trinity from 1605 to 1648, who became known as 'the Patriarch of Dorchester'. His powerful preaching and piety made Dorchester one of the mostly strongly Puritan towns in the country. Thomas Fuller, the eminent seventeenth-century historian and biographer, who became the incumbent of Broadwindsor in 1634, describes John White's influence in Dorchester and further afield in the memorable phrase, '. . . he stains all other men's lives with the clearness of his own'. One of John White's most remarkable achievements was his early interest in the idea of a colony in the New World where men might find the religious freedom denied them in England. He was thus concerned with the setting up of the Dorchester Company to promote such a scheme in 1623, and in various early unsuccessful attempts to found a colony in Massachusetts. Finally in 1630 he was instrumental in sending out from Plymouth a party of Puritans, many of them Dorset men and women, to settle in New Dorchester, Massachusetts. Other parties followed during the next few years.

During the early successes of the Royalists in the Civil War, Puritan sympathisers among the clergy suffered, notably John White of Dorchester whose library was burnt by the king's troops. Later, when Parliament gained the upper hand, some seventy of the royalist clergy of Dorset were ejected from their livings. Similar ejections followed the end of Puritan rule and the return of the monarchy in 1660. The Act of Uniformity (1662) prohibited the Puritan clergy from retaining their benefices, and in Dorset nearly a hundred clergy resigned as a result of this Act. Among them was John Wesley, vicar of Winterborne Whitchurch and grandfather of the great religious leader of the next century. He was a prominent Puritan minister, and in 1661 was reported 'for diabolically railing in the pulpit against the late King and his posterity, and praising Cromwell'. After the Act of 1662 he refused to use the Book of Common Prayer and was, with some difficulty, expelled from his benefice. Altogether more than half of the parishes in the county suffered from ejections of one kind or another during this whole period.

The time of the Civil War and Commonwealth saw a remarkable growth in Dorset of Congregational and Quaker churches. George Fox visited the county in 1655 and had large meetings at Poole, Dorchester and Weymouth. By 1668 there were sixteen Quaker meeting places. George Fox's final visit to the county was in 1668, when he came to Ryme Intrinseca which, interestingly, had a strong Puritan tradition dating back to Elizabeth's reign. Fox records that he came 'to one Harris his house, where he had a large Men's Meeting'. This was the house of George Harris, whose family had lived in Ryme for many years. After the Act of Toleration of 1689, a permanent Quaker Meeting house and graveyard was established at Ryme and also at a dozen other places in the county. Before 1689, however, Quakers were subjected to a great deal of persecution for their beliefs and their unconventional behaviour. In 1662, for example, no less than 200 Quakers are said to have been imprisoned in the county for various offences.

Perhaps because Nonconformity was early established in Dorset, particularly in the towns, the disputes and rancour of the seventeenth century did not continue into the eighteenth; when Defoe visited the county in the early eighteenth century he was greatly impressed by the religious toleration in Dorchester:

> . . . Dorchester is indeed a pleasant agreeable town to live in, and where I thought the people seem'd less divided into factions and parties, than in other places; for though here are divisions and the people are not all of one mind, either as to religion, or politicks, yet they did not seem to separate with so much animosity as in other places: Here I saw the Church of England clergymen, and the Dissenting minister, or preacher drinking tea together, and conversing with civility and good neighbourhood, like catholick Christians, and men of a catholick, and extensive charity: a man that coveted a retreat in this world might as agreeably spend his time, and as well in Dorchester, as in any town I know in England.

The Church of England in the Archdeaconry of Dorset during the eighteenth century, shared in the general lack of zeal or 'enthusiasm' which characterised the Anglican church during this period, though there appear to have been comparatively few instances of scandalous neglect. Sources for church history in the county during the eighteenth century are not numerous. Many of the church records of this period were destroyed, either in the great fire at Blandford in 1731 in which the documents of the Archdeacon's court perished, or in the fire at the Bishops' Palace and Library in Bristol in 1831, which was caused by the Reform riots in the City. One interesting source which has survived, however, is a large notebook of Bishop Secker who was bishop of Bristol from 1735 to 1737, and who made notes on the parishes in his diocese, the churches, incumbents, etc. These notes were continued after his time, particularly by Bishop Thomas Newton, who stayed an unusually long time in the diocese, 1761 to 1782. The general impression from these notes is a largely favourable one. There was certainly a great deal of pluralism and non-residence among the beneficed clergy, but generally a curate was appointed to serve the parish, though the curates were themselves sometimes pluralists and non-resident. The vicar of Hilton in 1766, for example, Mr Lemoin, resided at Plymouth where he kept a school and had a small benefice. His curate was also the rector of Melcombe Horsey. The rector of Tarrant Hinton lived at Bremmer in Hampshire; his curate who was also his nephew, was rector of Hammoon besides being curate of Tarrant Hinton and Tarrant Monkton. At Iwerne Minster in 1766, the Bishop noted that the vicar 'lives at Offenham near Evesham. Mr Rumney of Blandford takes care of the church for half a guinea each Sunday.' The rector of Chilfrome and Wraxall lived in Sussex and 'has not resided since his institution'. His curate was also the vicar of Bradpole. Such arrangements were of course common throughout the church of the time. Most parishes had at least one service each Sunday, often two with catechism for the children during the afternoons. Communion services were generally held four times a year.

In view of the isolation and loneliness which many of the clergy in remote Dorset parishes must have experienced, and the fact that there was no provision for clerical retirement because of old age or infirmity, it is perhaps surprising that so few instances of neglect or eccentricity are recorded in the bishop's notebook. At Gussage All Saints the vicar, Mr Rees Prosser, is said to be 'very wicked and drunken'. He was severely reproved and further measures against him were to be taken if there was any further fault. At Hampreston the rector did not reside because the parsonage house was burnt down some years previously, and although money and materials had been given to him in order to rebuild the house, nothing had been done, and he had sold the material. Mr Wetham, rector of Buckhorn Weston did not reside in the parish and 'complains much of ill-health, tho' he looks the picture of health itself'. At Milborne St Andrew the vicar, 'drank too much formerly, is now mad'. At Wareham the former rector was said to have been a lunatic, and this had greatly increased the number of dissenters. In general the church buildings are said to be in good repair; or only minor faults are noticed, which are later said to have been put right. This is rather surprising in view of the poor condition of some of the church buildings later; conditions which often necessitated very drastic restorations. Only two churches are noted as being in very bad condition. Wyke Regis is said to be so bad that it is dangerous to enter it, and Radipole church is noted as being 'decayed and weak and kept together by iron cramps'.

The older forms of dissent had many adherents in a large number of the parishes. At Bridport, Lyme Regis, Charmouth and neighbouring areas there were a large number of Presbyterians. Around Chideock, Lulworth and Marnhull there were many Catholics; and at Marnhull 'a house to which there is a great resort of Papists on Sundays'. At Weymouth and Melcombe Regis the whole Corporation and most of the town are said to be dissenters. Very large numbers of dissenters are also mentioned at Wyke Regis and Wareham. It is of interest that at Lyme Regis the old Puritan arrangement of the chancel survived and 'The Communion table [is] not set altarwise but with a rail quite round it in the middle of the Chancel'.

Evidence of the continuing strength of the Nonconformist churches in eighteenth- and early-nineteenth-century Dorset is still to be seen in the size and distinction of the surviving meeting houses. There are many examples in the county, including the early Quaker meeting houses at Bridport and Poole, the fine eighteenth-century Congregational churches at Lyme Regis, Wareham, Poole and elsewhere, and the Unitarian chapel at Bridport. Probably because of the strength of the dissenting churches in the county, Methodism made only slow headway. John Wesley only preached at all frequently at Shaftesbury, where he achieved comparatively little success, and in his journal wrote in 1766 of 'cold, uncomfortable Shaftesbury', and again in 1771 he wrote, 'I scarce know a town in England where so much preaching has been to so little purpose.' Charles Wesley had visited Dorset as early as 1746 and stayed for some days on the Island of Portland, but even here, although a Methodist society was established, it did not become really strong until the 1790s. Methodism only really began to flourish in the county during the nineteenth century, as is witnessed by the very large number of chapels built in the Dorset villages during the century. Returns made to Parliament in 1835–6 show that there were then 233 parishes in Dorset for which separate returns were made and there were 273 dissenting meeting houses and Roman Catholic chapels in the county. Of these the Methodists were a minority; far more numerous were the Independents and Baptists. Of the clergy of the Church of England, about half the incumbents were non-resident for various reasons, though most of the non-residents employed curates to conduct the services.

In 1836 Dorset was transferred from the diocese of Bristol, in which it had been included since 1542, to become once more part of the diocese of Salisbury. This led to a very considerable revival of church life in the county, under the impetus of two energetic bishops, Dennison who was bishop of Salisbury from 1837 to 1854, and Kerr Hamilton who was bishop from 1854 to 1869. This revival is marked by a great spate of church building and restoration in the county during the nineteenth century. A Parliamentary Return of 1876 lists all the churches rebuilt or restored at a cost of more than £500 since 1840, and in the archdeaconry of Dorset 158 such churches are listed, including many on which very large sums had been spent. Amongst the many churches which had involved heavy expenditure are the following:

Sherborne Abbey	£31,715	Long Crichel	£14,000
Weymouth, Holy Trinity	£12,050	Fontmell Magna	£12,000
Wimborne Minster	£10,211	Corfe Castle	£10,000
Milton Abbas	£ 9,000	Portland St Peter	£ 8,000
Weymouth St John	£ 7,500	Bere Regis	£ 5,806

There are many other examples of such very large sums spent on church building and restoration in the county during this period —striking evidence both of the wealth available, and of the piety and concern for church buildings which is such a marked feature of the nineteenth century.

SELECT BIBLIOGRAPHY

J. Berkeley	*Lulworth and the Welds* (1971)
J. H. Bettey	'Sir John Tregonwell of Milton Abbey' (*Dorset Proceedings*, vol 90, 1969)
J. Brocklebank	*Affpuddle* (1968)
J. Fowler	*Medieval Sherborne* (1951)
R. Lloyd	*Dorset Elizabethans* (1967)
J. Newman and N. Pevsner	*The Buildings of England: Dorset* (1972)
R.C.H.M.	*Dorset*
Victoria County History	*Dorset*, vol II (1908)

Chapter 7 POLITICAL, MILITARY AND MARITIME HISTORY

THE political and military history of the county before the Norman Conquest has already been discussed in Chapters 1 and 2. The Norman Conquest and the imposition of Norman rule which followed was marked by a spate of castle building in Dorset, and castles or motte and bailey fortifications were erected at a number of places, including Wareham, Corfe, Sherborne, Portland, Dorchester, Sturminster Newton, Shaftesbury, Chelborough and Powerstock. Dorset saw a good deal of the fighting during the Civil War in the reign of Stephen, and the Dorset castles were important factors in the war. Several of the most powerful supporters of the Empress Matilda possessed extensive lands in Dorset, including her half-brother Robert, earl of Gloucester, Baldwin de Redvers and William de Mohun. The war probably caused more misery and destruction in the county than any other incident in its history. In 1142, for example, Stephen attacked Wareham Castle which was strongly defended by Robert, earl of Gloucester, and during the unsuccessful siege a contemporary chronicler records that Stephen 'raged cruelly everywhere with fire and sword . . . pillaging and plundering everything that came his way'. Dorset saw many such incidents during the troubled years of the mid-twelfth century.

King John on his constant travels around the country spent a good deal of time in Dorset, hunting in Cranborne Chase, the Blackmoor Vale and Powerstock Forest, and he spent large sums of money on strengthening the royal castles at Dorchester and Corfe, and on the royal hunting lodge which he had built at Gillingham, of which the moat and earthworks remain now forlornly deserted in a field. He also used Corfe Castle as a prison, and as a stronghold and refuge for himself in some of the most difficult periods of his troubled reign. Corfe was later to be used again as a prison in 1327 for Edward II before he was taken to Berkeley Castle in Gloucestershire where he was murdered.

During the later Middle Ages several of the Dorset towns each sent two members to Parliament. The four oldest Dorset boroughs, Dorchester, Bridport, Shaftesbury and Wareham, sent two members each from the time of Edward I, and later, members were also returned for Lyme Regis, Weymouth, Melcombe Regis and Poole. From the reign of Elizabeth members were also returned from Corfe Castle. There were thus nine Parliamentary boroughs with eighteen members, in addition to the two county members, right up to the reform of the whole system in 1832, since even after the union of Weymouth and Melcombe Regis in 1571 they continued to be represented by four members of Parliament, elected by all the freeholders. Until the sixteenth century, membership of Parliament was not a duty much sought after, since it involved a long and arduous journey and provided few compensations. The county and borough members throughout the Middle Ages are, therefore, drawn not from the great and often non-resident landowners, but from the gentry who lived in the county and from many of the families which were to become important during the sixteenth century. Names such as Maybank, Turberville, Newburgh, Peverell, Sifrewast, Matravers, etc occur again and again.

In the fourteenth and fifteenth centuries Dorset suffered very severely from the Black Death, which has already been discussed in Chapter 3, and also from repeated French and Spanish raids on the coastal towns and villages. Melcombe Regis, for example, was burnt in 1377 and again in 1380, and Bridport, Lyme Regis and Poole suffered similar attacks. In 1401 the Patent Rolls of King Henry IV record that Lyme is 'so wasted and burned by attacks of the sea and assaults of the King's enemies and frequent pestilences that scarcely a twentieth part of it is now inhabited'. In 1469 a list and valuation of the possessions of the monastery at Abbotsbury explains that the low value of the manor of Portesham is 'because few tenants dare dwell there for fear of the enemies of the King and the whole Kingdom of England frequently arriving and coming by sea there'. Bexington was burnt by the French in 1440 and the inhabitants were carried off as prisoners.

During the sixteenth century, when on several occasions there was again the threat of invasion by either France or Spain, Dorset was in the front line of defence. Henry VIII's scheme of fortification for the south coast involved two new castles in the county facing each other across Portland Roads—Sandsfoot and Portland. These were built during 1539–40 to protect the anchorage at Portland. Sandsfoot has almost completely disappeared, but the splendid castle at Portland survives and is an excellent and well-preserved example of the military architecture of the time. An inscription within the castle reads: 'God save King Henri the VIII of that name, and Prins Edward, begotten of Quene Jane, my Ladi Mari that goodli virgin, and the Ladi Elizabeth so towardli, with the Kinges honorable counselers.' An important and spectacular sea-battle was fought off Portland on 2 August 1588, during the progress of the Spanish Armada up the English Channel. The Spanish fleet was becalmed as it neared Portland Bill on the evening of Monday 1 August, and on the following day a very fierce engagement took place between the Armada and the English ships. The battle was fought close to the land and was clearly visible to the watchers on the coast. Martin Frobisher, commanding the *Triumph*, the largest ship in either fleet, cleverly made use of his knowledge of the coast by anchoring in the lee of Portland Bill from where he was able to inflict considerable damage on the Spanish ships which were exposed both to the fire of the English and to the navigational perils of the Portland Race and the Shambles sand bank.

Dorset also played a very important part in the Civil War, although no major battle was fought in the county. The strategic importance of the county for both sides in the conflict was very great, since not only did it have a number of very well fortified castles and strongholds, but it also formed an important link between London and the royalist West. Moreover, the Dorset ports could provide valuable contact with the Continent for the King's forces. In the years before the war broke out, the policies followed by Charles I and his ministers had been as unpopular in Dorset as elsewhere. As shown in Chapter 6, many of the towns were strongly Puritan in sympathy; for example, Poole, Dorchester under its zealous minister John White, and Beaminster. Such places were greatly angered by the imposition of 'ship money', the billeting of soldiers in private houses, by the religious policies of Archbishop Laud, and all the other grievances which led up to the outbreak of war in 1642. The 'ship money' tax became increasingly difficult to collect in the county. In 1636 the Sheriff, John Freke, wrote that the tax was paid 'like drops of blood', and in 1640 when some cattle were seized by the Crown because of their owners' refusal to pay the tax, no one would buy them when they were offered for sale at Blandford Forum. There were many similar incidents illustrating the unpopularity of the royal policy. When the war finally began in 1642, however, much of the old loyalty to the Crown reasserted itself. The great majority of large landowners were mainly royalist in sympathy, including the two great Catholic families, the Arundels of Chideock and the Welds who had recently come to Lulworth. Most of the inhabitants of Sherborne, Blandford, Corfe, Portland, Weymouth and Bridport supported the king, while Dorchester, Poole, Wareham, Lyme Regis and Melcombe Regis were Parliamentarian. Dorchester, which held the county militia's supply of ammunition, supported Parliament very strongly and exercised great influence in the county; Clarendon in his *History of the Rebellion* called it 'the magazine from whence the other places were supplied with the principles of Rebellion'. The royal army from the west advanced through Dorset in 1643 and achieved great success. Although the royalists could not make any headway against the stubborn resistance of Lyme Regis or Poole, the rest of the county was in the king's hands. Even at Dorchester, where elaborate defences had been prepared and large sums of money had been spent on fortifying the town, the inhabitants surrendered to the royal forces without a shot being fired. Lyme Regis, however, continued to stand firm against the Crown, and another unsuccessful attempt was made to capture the town in 1644 by a royalist army under Prince Maurice. During the siege of Lyme, some of the royal forces were garrisoned at Beaminster, and on Palm Sunday 1644 a dispute amongst the king's soldiers, possibly between the Cornish and the French contingents, led to a fire being started, and a contemporary account records that 'the whole towne was all destroyed in Two Hours; and those Goods for the most part which were carried out of the Fire, were carried away by the soldiers'. A leading part in the defence of Lyme Regis was taken by Robert Blake who was later to distinguish himself as an admiral when he commanded the English fleet which defeated the Dutch at the battle off Portland in 1653. Blake's two great successes, one military, the other naval, were thus obtained within a very few miles of each other.

In June 1644 a large Parliamentary army under the earl of Essex captured Weymouth and relieved the siege of Lyme Regis. Later the same year, King Charles and his army passed through the county after their victorious campaign in Cornwall. The passing and repassing of armies caused a great deal of damage, plundering, requisitioning of goods and the total dislocation of ordinary life, apart from the destruction caused by actual fighting. By 1645 most people in Dorset were heartily sick of war, and there occurred one of the most interesting and curious episodes in the history of the county. This was the rising of the 'Clubmen', a group which claimed to be neutral in the struggle between king and Parliament and were concerned only to protect themselves and their property against the damage caused by both sides. Such risings were not unknown elsewhere, in Somerset, Wiltshire and Herefordshire for example, but the Dorset Clubmen seem to have been the most numerous and important of such groups of protesters. The governor of Poole, Colonel John Bingham, reported to Parliament on 1 March 1645 that there were '. . . near 1,000 countrymen gotten into a body with guns and clubs to resist the French and Irish amongst the Cavaliers'. Other estimates give their numbers as nearer 4,000, though no doubt these reports were exaggerated.

The Dorset Clubmen were drawn from the yeomen, farmers, tradesmen and others who had suffered most grievously in the disturbances and in the passing of armies through the county. There were also a few younger sons of gentry families, and a number of clergy, many of whom were opposed to the religious changes being discussed by Parliament. After the great defeat of the royal army at Naseby in June 1645, it was the Parliamentary army that the Dorset Clubmen saw as the greatest threat to their lives and property. During the summer of 1645 they made a number of attempts to hinder the Parliamentary forces in the county, and in particular they directed their attention to the army under Sir Thomas Fairfax which on 2 August 1645 began the siege of Sherborne Castle. Some of the Clubmen established themselves at Shaftesbury from where they were dispersed by Parliamentary forces commanded by Cromwell himself. Another group encamped in the Iron Age earthwork on Hambledon Hill, and proved very difficult to dislodge. On 4 August 1645 Cromwell found nearly 2,000 Clubmen in this strong position on the hill-top, and after an unsuccessful attempt to negotiate with them, finally defeated them by an attack from the rear. About a dozen of the Clubmen were killed, and some 300 taken prisoners and locked up in the church at Iwerne Courtney (Shroton), where Cromwell lectured them and made them all promise to be well behaved in future, before they were released. Cromwell wrote that they '... are poor silly creatures ... [and] they promise to be very dutiful for time to come, and will be hanged before they come out again'. The whole episode of the Clubmen, while not materially affecting the course of events in the Civil War, remains a remarkable example of protest by the ordinary people of Dorset whose feelings are generally hidden by the march of the great and historic events which affected them.

On 15 August 1645, Sherborne Castle was taken by the Parliamentary forces after a brave but hopelessly prolonged defence under the governor, Sir Lewis Dyve. This marked the beginning of the end of royalist resistance in Dorset. In February 1646 Corfe Castle finally fell to the Parliamentary forces after a very long resistance, under the indomitable Lady Bankes. The defeat was due to the treachery of one of the garrison, Lieutenant Colonel Thomas Pittman. He managed to get a considerable force of Parliamentary soldiers let in to the castle by pretending that they were royalist reinforcements. Once inside, they attacked the defenders and enabled the rest of the Parliamentary forces to enter the castle, which was soon forced to surrender. Finally in April 1646 Portland Castle was surrendered, and Dorset was completely under the control of Parliament. After their surrender, the defences at Sherborne and Corfe were destroyed by order of Parliament, leaving both as total ruins. Enough remains at Corfe, however, to show that it was one of the most notable castles in England. Situated as it is in such a strategic place, it remains still tremendously impressive and of great architectural importance.

After the battle of Worcester on 3 September 1651, Prince Charles sought refuge in Dorset from the Parliamentary forces who were scouring England for him. He was sheltered for a time at Francis Wyndham's house at Trent, which then was just over the border in Somerset, and later went on to Bridport from where he hoped to obtain a passage to France. The plan fell through at the last moment but Charles spent a very anxious night at Charmouth, and only escaped capture because the parson, Bartholomew Wesley, great-great grandfather of John Wesley, to whom the ostler at the inn reported his suspicions about the identity of the traveller, did not take any action until the fugitive had gone. Charles meanwhile fled through Bridport, Broadwindsor and back again to Trent, only narrowly escaping detection on several occasions. Finally he left Trent again on 6 October 1651 and was eventually able to get a ship from Shoreham.

During the period of Parliamentary rule in England, Dorset was governed by a Standing Committee. The Minute Books of this committee have been printed for the period 1646–50, and provide a complete account of the administration of the county at this time, since the committee controlled all aspects of government from administering and disposing of the estates of royalist delinquents to minute supervision of the ecclesiastical affairs of the county, the appointments of ministers, parish clerks, registrars of marriages, repair of churches and a host of other matters. Inevitably, the minute and detailed supervision of daily life was not always very popular, particularly in an area where there had been a good deal of royalist sympathy. When Charles II was finally restored to the throne in May 1660 there was great rejoicing in many of the towns and villages of Dorset. At Sherborne, which had been particularly royalist, the news of the king's restoration was received with immense joy, and a contemporary report describes the scene, 'Sir John Strangways read the Proclamation ... after which followed shouts and acclamations and several volleys; the Conduit ran wine two daies together, the loyal Town being transported with the glorious triumph of that joyful day.'

The next event of great national importance in which Dorset was closely involved was the Monmouth Rebellion. If the episode of the Clubmen is the most curious in Dorset history, the events following the landing of the Duke of Monmouth at Lyme Regis in June 1685 are certainly the most tragic and pathetic. Lyme Regis, with its Puritan tradition and memories of its heroic resistance to the royal forces during the Civil War, received Monmouth with great rejoicing as the Protestant saviour, and he stayed at Lyme for a week while recruits poured in to join his army. In Dorset, as in Somerset, however, Monmouth's recruits were almost entirely from the lower classes, the nonconformist small freeholders, yeoman farmers, artisans in the woollen industry from Dorset and Devon, small traders and craftsmen from Lyme Regis and district. Not many of the well-to-do joined his ranks, though a few younger sons did so. On 18 June 1685 Monmouth with his motley and untrained army marched away to Taunton, and to the crushing defeat which awaited him and his unfortunate followers at Sedgemoor less than a month after his landing. Monmouth himself fled from the battle of Sedgemoor, and was finally captured, disguised as a shepherd, on Horton Heath in the east of Dorset, while attempting to reach the coast. After the Rebellion came the terrible retribution. In September 1685 Judge Jeffreys came to Dorchester, and nearly 350 men were tried for their part in the rebellion, of whom no less than 251 were sentenced to death for their part in the rising. The proceedings at Dorchester were even more dreadful and 'bloody' than anywhere else on Jeffreys' tour through the South West, and a higher proportion of those sentenced at Dorchester were actually executed; seventy-four of them were executed, and the hangings and the dreadful scenes that accompanied them took place almost immediately, and while the Assizes were still in progress. Perhaps even more terrible than the executions, and the aspect of the whole episode that has left its mark most clearly in folk memory in the area, was the horrid display of the heads and quarters of the unfortunate men who were executed in towns and villages throughout the area. The accounts for several Dorset parishes contain references to expenditure on this grisly business, for the executions were distributed all over the county. For example, the Weymouth accounts contain the following entries:

> 14th October 1685
> To a bill of disbursements for ye Gallows,
> Burning and Boyling ye Rebels executed by
> Order att this Towne £16-4-8
> 20th November 1685
> Paid for new setting up a post with the
> quarters of ye Rebells att Waymouth
> Towne-End £ 0-1-6

The men who had followed Monmouth were, it must be remembered, for the most part simple unlettered country folk, men from the farms of the Marshwood Vale, from the Puritan-minded towns like Lyme, Beaminster and Dorchester, who had followed Monmouth in an excess of religious zeal and out of concern for the maintenance of their liberties, and above all for the Protestant religion. Their idealism was no doubt misplaced, but could hardly have deserved the dreadful fate which it so quickly incurred.

Besides those who were executed, a great many more were transported to the West Indies. During the autumn of 1685, several shiploads of rebels left from Weymouth, Bristol and elsewhere. Eighty men left Weymouth on the *Betty* of London, another sixty-seven went by the *Jamaica Merchant*, a further ninety-one sailed on the ironically named *Happy Return* of Poole. All these were bound for Barbados, at that time the wealthiest and most important British colony in the West Indies. Amongst those who were transported from Dorset was Azariah Pinney, one of the few well-to-do persons who had joined Monmouth. He was a member of a long-established west Dorset family, and his father, John Pinney, was the minister of Broadwindsor during the Commonwealth. The family possessed land in Bettiscombe, and also had a considerable lace-making business. When Azariah was sentenced for his part in the Monmouth affair, his family were able to use their wealth and influence to secure better treatment for him, and he was transported as a free emigrant. Once in the West Indies he was free to act as agent for other members of the family, selling lace and a variety of other goods, and building up a substantial business. Eventually he became a plantation-owner on a large scale and established a secure fortune. Like so many others, a few days under Monmouth's standard dramatically changed Azariah Pinney's whole life, though unlike him, few of his fellow rebels derived any profit from their involvement in the rising.

Apart from the interruption caused by the Civil War, the machinery of local government in the county continued without any major changes throughout the seventeenth, eighteenth and early nineteenth centuries. By far the most important officials in the local administration were the Justices of the Peace. They were appointed from the local gentry and dealt with a vast amount of legal and administrative business either singly or in Quarter Sessions. The latter were held in various places throughout the county, generally at Sherborne, Shaftesbury, Blandford and Bridport, and occasionally at some other places, with adjournments at Dorchester. Dorchester, although it was the Assize town, did not become the administrative centre of the county until the nineteenth century. The surviving Quarter Sessions Minutes and Orders give a fascinating picture of life in the county, for the justices dealt with a bewildering range of subjects. The records contain information on the licensing of public houses, religious meeting houses, gamekeepers, carriers, etc, on fires in Dorset towns and villages and the attempts which were made to relieve the sufferers, on rogues and vagabonds, wounded soldiers and other travellers through the county, as well as information on the constant problems of crime and its punishment. The justices were also concerned with unlawful games and plays, and, for example, they were involved when in 1630 a travelling puppet theatre arrived at Beaminster having already played at other towns in the county. At Beaminster the worthy Puritan townsfolk complained to the justices that they were subjected to 'certaine blasphemous shewes and sights . . . poppet playing at Beaminster, not only in the daye time but also late at night'. It was alleged that some apprentices and others stayed up so late watching the puppets that they could not work the next day. Quarter Sessions duly ordered the puppet show to depart out of the county. The justices' duties also included the care of the county roads and bridges, the licensing of turnpikes, and settling the numerous and protracted disputes between parishes as to their respective responsibility for orphans, illegitimate children and other unfortunates. Under the Local Government Act of 1888, the County Council came into existence and took over the administration of the county.

Until the Reform Act of 1832 Dorset continued to return twenty members to Parliament, two for the county and two each from the nine boroughs. For the county elections the right to vote was possessed by those with freehold land worth annually 40s. In the boroughs the voting qualification varied considerably, and during the eighteenth century the elections in the little boroughs of Dorset were accompanied by a great deal of corruption, bribery and intimidation, and there were many disputes over election results. Poole with its important overseas trade had a long tradition of turbulence in political matters. The right to vote rested with little more than a hundred freemen so that bribery and corruption could find a ready ground, and there were a succession of scandals. The twin boroughs of Weymouth and Melcombe Regis also became notorious for the corruption of their elections. For much of the eighteenth century the twin boroughs were dominated by the influence of Bubb Dodington, the son of a Weymouth apothecary, who inherited a vast fortune from his uncle, and spent his life in political intrigue and manipulation. He used his great wealth to complete the enormous mansion his uncle had begun at Eastbury, near Blandford Forum, and from his residence there he interested himself particularly in his home town, and spent money unstintingly to ensure his control of the borough members of Parliament. When finally in the last year of his life he was granted a peerage by George III in 1761, he took the title of Baron Melcombe of Melcombe Regis. Political corruption and manipulation of elections was also frequently alleged at Corfe, Shaftesbury, and elsewhere in the county.

The Reform Act of 1832 began the process of re-organising the parliamentary representation of the county. The little borough of Corfe lost both its members and ceased to be a borough; Wareham, Lyme and Shaftesbury were reduced to one member each; Weymouth and Melcombe Regis had their four seats reduced to two. A further Act in 1867 deprived Lyme of its remaining member, and reduced all the other boroughs to one member each. In 1885 the whole system was changed and the county was divided into four divisions each with an MP. At the same time voting rights were extended to include agricultural workers, so that for the first time most of the male population of the county could now be said to be represented in Parliament.

At the end of the eighteenth century Dorset once more found itself in the forefront of national defence, this time against the threat of invasion by a Napoleonic army, and the most elaborate arrangements were made in case an enemy force should land. The coastal defences at Poole, Swanage, Portland, Weymouth and elsewhere were strengthened and volunteer forces were raised to supplement the militia and the regular army. The Dorset Yeomanry was founded in 1794, and many of the Dorset towns had their own volunteer troops, often with their own uniforms, such as the Puddletown Volunteer Light Infantry, the Evershot Volunteers, the Beaminster Loyal Town Volunteers, and many others. Along the coast parties of Sea Fencibles or coastal defenders were formed, such as the Royal Portland Legion. The whole operation and atmosphere is irresistibly reminiscent of the similar situation in 1940. The most complicated and painstaking arrangements were also worked out for signalling the arrival of any enemy force, and for evacuating the whole coastal area. All inhabitants, cattle, goods and anything which might be useful to the enemy were to be moved inland, and immensely detailed and elaborate plans were drawn up to ensure that this was carried out and that everyone knew where to go and what route to take. The whole atmosphere and mood of the time is perhaps best summed up in Thomas Hardy's novel *The Trumpet Major*, with its troops of soldiers everywhere, the king and the royal family at Weymouth, the fears and excitements, the fleet at anchor off Portland, the feeling of fearful anticipation. There were several false alarms. One was described by the *Sherborne Journal* on 8 April 1799:

> Monday evening about ten o'clock an express arrived from a neighbouring signal house to the Commanding Officer at Bridport stating that an enemy was actually landing in the west . . . The drums immediately beat to arms, the three companies of Bridport Volunteers assembled with amazing alacrity and remained steadily under arms the whole night anxious to march where-ever their services may be required . . . The loyalty of each corps cannot be too much applauded . . . About seven in the morning intelligence was received that a mistake had been made at the signal house.

At the height of the invasion scare in May 1804, the signal station on the Verne at Portland gave a false alarm during thick fog which created a great panic throughout the county, and led to grave fears for the safety of George III who was staying at Weymouth.

Another aspect of the war conditions was the activities of the Press Gang along the coast. An example of this occurred early on the morning of 2 April 1803 when a Press Gang from the frigate *Aigle* landed at Portland and captured two men. A large crowd of Portlanders quickly gathered and a scuffle commenced. The Press Gang opened fire and three Portlanders were killed and others injured. The ship's officers were arrested and lodged in

Dorchester gaol on a charge of murder, but were eventually acquitted on the grounds that they had acted in self-defence.

Most of the great development of military and government establishments in Dorset has taken place during the twentieth century, but one important development which took place in the nineteenth century was the construction of the great naval harbour and base at Portland. The increasing size of the ships of the Royal Navy meant that they could no longer enter the smaller ports, and it was therefore decided to construct a deep-water anchorage at some point midway between Portsmouth and Plymouth. Portland was chosen for this harbour of refuge, and in 1847 an Act of Parliament was passed to enable work to start on the massive breakwater. This was built by convict labour, and a prison was established on the island to house the prisoners. The convicts hewed stone from the quarries and this was sent by an inclined plane down to the shore and used to construct the breakwater. By 1872 Albert Edward, Prince of Wales, could perform the official opening ceremony, though a good deal more has been built since that time. In addition to the breakwater, a great citadel was built on the Verne, the highest point of the island, to guard the harbour. Today the prison has become a Borstal Institution while the Verne Citadel is now used as a prison.

In 1844 the county boundaries were redrawn slightly, and a few long-standing anomalies were cleared up. Stockland and Dalwood in the far west which had been part of Dorset, but which were geographically in Devon, were officially declared part of Devon, while Thorncombe parish, which includes the site of the former great Cistercian Abbey of Forde, and which had hitherto been part of Devon was now transferred to Dorset. Holwell parish, which by a curious anomaly had previously been an outlying part of Somerset, although some miles from the county boundary, was now declared to be part of Dorset. A further tidying up of boundaries occurred in 1896 and this transferred the parishes of Trent, Poyntington, Sandford Orcas, Goathill and Seaborough from Somerset to Dorset, while Chardstock and Hawkchurch passed to Devon and Wambrook to Somerset.

SELECT BIBLIOGRAPHY

A. R. Bailey	*The Civil War in Dorset* (1910)
C. D. Curtis	*Blake: General at Sea* (1934)
B. Little	*The Monmouth Episode* (1956)
R. Lloyd	*Dorset Elizabethans* (1967)
C. H. Mayo (ed)	*The Minute Books of the Dorset Standing Committee 1646–50* (1902)
R. Pares	*A West India Fortune* (1950)
Victoria County History	*Dorset*, vol II (1908)

Chapter 8 THE PEOPLE

It is very difficult to get any very intimate impression of the great majority of people who lived in Dorset before the sixteenth or seventeenth centuries. We can obtain little idea of their thoughts and ideas from the remaining records, though the more formal records of their dealings with various authorities—Church, State and manorial courts, etc—survive in considerable quantities. It is certain that life for the majority was one of hard and unremitting toil, a constant struggle to grow enough food to sustain themselves and their families during the long winter months, at a time when the fertility of crops was low and when crops and animals as well as humans were ravaged by disease and were completely at the mercy of the weather. A number of very detailed accounts survive from the Middle Ages of the work demanded of the tenants on several of the manors in the county, and these show very clearly the great deal of time the peasant was expected to spend working on his lord's land before he could even start on his own work. For example, at the manor of Fontmell in 1135 the labour services on the demesne lands of the great nunnery of Shaftesbury amounted to as much as three days a week, as well as dues, payments and other services. At Little Piddle in 1288 the tenants paid a money rental and also worked for the lord of the manor at a variety of specified tasks throughout the year, ploughing, harrowing, weeding, mowing grass, carrying hay, reaping and carrying corn and threshing. Even when the labour services were commuted for a money rental, as happened widely in Dorset during the later Middle Ages, the burden on the peasant remained a heavy one. Moreover, many of the manors in the county were part of great estates or were owned by monastic houses, and the stewards of these great landowners would be likely to insist rigidly on the prompt payment of rents and the performance of labour services.

A splendidly detailed 'custumal', or account of customs and practices, survives from 1250 for the manor of Burton, part of the parish of Marnhull. The manor belonged to Glastonbury Abbey, and the custumal sets out the 'Rents and customs owing yearly to the lord Abbot of Glastonbury'. A good idea of the annual round of services required can be obtained by taking as an example one tenant, Robert Tac. He was among the more prosperous and substantial tenants, farming one virgate, ie about forty acres of arable and having grazing rights on the commons. For this he paid 6s in money rent, and was bound to work for the abbot for at least some part of several days each week. His year was closely regulated by the annual round of saints' days, feasts and holy days. For example: 'he ought to work (on the lord's land) every day from the feast of St Peter ad Vincula (29 June) to the feast of St Michael (29 September) excepting feast days and Saturdays'. He was also expected to take the lord's corn to Glastonbury when required: 'he ought for the whole year to carry the lord's corn with his beast as well from Niweton [another Glastonbury manor in Sturminster Newton parish] as Burton to Glastonbury or elsewhere at the lord's will'. One wonders when he got any time to work his own forty acres.

The custumal also lays down the tenants' rights and privileges. Robert Tac was, for example, entitled to a dinner on Christmas Day—'. . . the lord to find him food on Christmas Day, to wit bread, cheese, pottage and two dishes of meat'. The tenant, however, had to provide his own plates and so on, and even the wood for the fire: 'And he shall take with him a plate, mug and napkin if he wishes to eat off a cloth, and he shall bring a faggot of brushwood to cook his food, unless he would have it raw.'

With this constant burden of toil, most of the great national events must have been for the majority of people no more than a distant rumour. Local happenings were much more memorable. When examined on oath concerning the date of the baptism of the lord of the manor, John Arundel (in order to establish his true age and the legality of his inheritance) the villagers of Sturminster Marshall could remember a wealth of detail. The baptism took place about 1408, and they were questioned about it at an inquiry held at Blandford some twenty-one years later in 1429. It was certainly an eventful day. Walter Russell remembered that he had carried two pots full of wine into the church for the refreshment of the godfathers and the godmother at the baptism. Perhaps others also had some of the wine for John Hekford stated that one Robert Roo had died suddenly in the church and Richard Pylke remembered that his father was seized with paralysis on that day, and John Garland recalled that he had broken his right arm by falling in the road on his way home from the church. Other witnesses also recollected a mass of detail concerning the events of the day, then twenty-one years ago.

It was a small, isolated and predominantly rural society. Most of the inhabitants of the county lived in little communities like the manor of Bincombe, the tiny village set under Bincombe Hill with magnificent views over Weymouth Bay. The manor belonged to the little priory of Frampton, a dependent cell of the great Norman abbey of St Stephen at Caen. At Bincombe in 1376 there were about twenty-five tenants, most of them having no more than a dozen acres of arable land each, together with grazing rights for their sheep and cattle on the hilly downland pasture, still dotted with a remarkable number of barrows, 'Celtic' fields, and other evidence of early settlement. The arable land was in three great fields around the village, North, South and Middle fields. These survived until 1827 and extensive remains of them may still be seen.

The tenants' lives were regulated by the extremely detailed customs of the manor, so precisely set out that today they occupy nine closely printed pages. These set out exactly what services the tenants were to provide, when grazing could commence on each part of the commons, the work to be done on the lord's land and the privileges of the tenants. Each was to receive a dinner on Christmas Day, and was to be provided with food if he journeyed to Frampton with corn or wool for the priory. Special privileges were laid down for the reeve, the shepherd and other officials, including the dairymaid—'The most honest woman of the whole town [ie community] ought to be dairymaid . . . and make the lord's cheese.'

Life centred around the regular procession of saints' days, and around the little twelfth-century church of the parish. Each of the tenants paid tithes and other dues to the church and to the vicar, including 'church scot', 'on the day of St Martin (11 November) they ought to pay of "chersete" [church scot] to wit 1 cock and 3 hens'. The attachment of the little community to their church is shown by the fact that in the fifteenth century it was partly rebuilt, the south wall of the nave was heightened and given new windows, and the west tower was added.

Apart from the tenants of the manors, and the townsfolk and traders in the ports and market towns, two other classes of society must be mentioned—the great landowners and the churchmen. The life of the landowners, such as the de Newburghs, the Strodes, Binghams, Clavells, Turbervilles, and other leading medieval families of the county differed little from that of their class and wealth all over the country. With them must be included also the abbots of the great Dorset abbeys and the abbesses of Shaftesbury and Tarrant Crawford, for these were in their own right amongst the richest and most extensive landowners in the county. For the most part they possessed very large estates, and their outlook and whole standard of life differed totally from that of the tenants on their manors. Of the churchmen, the lives of most of the parish clergy were but little different from that of the majority of their flock. Their educational attainments were perhaps a little higher and their interests somewhat wider, but they were equally dependent upon the soil for their livelihood and equally at the mercy of the agricultural uncertainties. Indeed, many farmed their own glebe land side by side with their congregations. There was also a very considerable number of men throughout the Middle Ages who were chantry priests or attached as secular priests to some ancient foundation such as the College of Wimborne

Minster, or to one of the various hospitals, or who were among the great number of monks and friars in the county.

By the sixteenth and seventeenth centuries much more material is available for obtaining some idea of the men and women who lived in Dorset. For example, the manor of Piddlehinton had since the reign of Henry VI belonged to Eton College, and there are a number of surveys conducted during the sixteenth century. The arable land of the manor was in three great open fields, each divided into strips. There was also meadow and pasture land, and extensive common grazing on the downland. The lands were divided between the tenant of the college's demesne land which amounted to 136 acres of arable, the rector who had forty acres of arable, 20 copyhold tenants each having 24 acres of arable and 10 copyholders each with 12 acres of arable. All these tenants also had grazing rights for their sheep and cattle on the downland in proportion to their arable holding, and the right to a portion of the meadow land for hay. There were in addition 16 cottagers who had only a house and garden, and a water mill at which all tenants were obliged to have their corn ground. The miller was entitled to 1/24th of all the corn he ground. By the sixteenth century most of the labour services had been commuted for a money payment, but the tenants at Piddlehinton were still obliged to work on the demesne lands at haymaking and to work another whole day in the corn harvest. They were also obliged to work each year on the Thursday in Whitsun week at cleaning and scouring the mill pond.

The manor of Cerne Abbas belonging to the Prince of Wales was surveyed in 1617 by the greatest land surveyors of their time, the Nordens, father and son. At Cerne there were more than 60 tenants, many of them tradesmen, occupying no more than a cottage and garden, or having only small amounts of land and no doubt combining farming with some craft or trade in the little market town. There was a weekly market held on Wednesday and three fairs each year. The arable land was in strips in three great fields around the town, and the tenants also had rights of grazing on Totcombe Hill, Rowden, Weam Hill and Trendle

Hill. The last mentioned is the hill on which the great figure of the Giant is cut, though there is no reference to him in the survey. The tenants also each had small portions of the town meadow for hay and grazing.

But the careful survey of the Nordens revealed that all was far from well in the manor, and that 'the towne is moste unorderlie governed and as unruiellie as if there were noe magistrates, for the officers are weake men . . .' Another major problem in the town was that: 'they that injoye the principall howses of the towne dwell from them and lett them to a masse of base people, meere mendicantes . . . One John Williams . . . hath a fayre house and hath put neer a dozen lowsey people in it and yet these howses stande in the principall parte of the towne, the market place'. Finally the Nordens reported that the Guild Hall had been allowed to get into such a bad state of repair 'and is now in that ruynous estate as none dare sitt in it, and eyther it muste be spedelie repayred or it will fall to the grounde'.

Similar surveys, though not always so precise or full as the Cerne one, exist for a great many Dorset manors for the sixteenth, seventeenth and eighteenth centuries, particularly for those great number of manors which formed part of some great estate where the records of estate management are more likely to have survived, like those of the Welds, the Digbys, the Strangways, and several others. The *Survey of Dorsetshire* written by Thomas Gerard of Trent c. 1630 gives much information, particularly about the gentry and the trading, merchant classes. The impression one gets is of a prosperous, busy society where wealth was increasing, where there were plenty of opportunities for the ambitious, and where the substantial farmers 'now beginne to encroach upon the Gentrie'. Gerard claims that the gentry families were 'for the most parte of antient descent', though in fact nearly half of them had come to prominence during the previous century, having profited by the opportunities for enrichment offered by the times. Such families included the Tregonwells, the Napiers, the Mellers and the Churchills; and within a few years several other prominent families were to appear in the county, having made their fortunes elsewhere, such as the Digbys, who obtained possession of Sir Walter Raleigh's estates and great house at Sherborne, the Cecils at Cranborne, the Bankes and the Welds.

Gerard comments also on the number of superb manor houses which had recently been erected or were being built. The prosperity of these years is still apparent from these houses, not only the manor houses, but also the innumerable farm houses, cottages and barns dating from this time. Houses built or greatly enlarged during the sixteenth and early seventeenth centuries include the great mansions, like the Strangways' huge house at Melbury, or the Horseys' house at Clifton Maybank, now largely demolished, or the Trenchards' house at Wolfeton. There are a host of others, the Strodes' house at Parnham, the Elizabethan house at Tyneham so unfortunately commandeered by the army, John Tregonwell's house at Anderson or the lovely house at Chantmarle built by Sir John Strode in the early seventeenth century and for which the fascinating building account survives. Loveliest of all perhaps is the Binghams' delectable house at Binghams Melcombe. Dorset is still extremely well endowed with manor houses.

Thomas Gerard was also impressed by the lively market towns of the county: Bridport, where he noted the great trade in hemp and flax and the brisk weekly market; Dorchester which 'hath encreased and flourished exceedinglie' and its growing population 'manie of which are Men of great Wealth'; Poole, which, although suffering from a temporary recession in Gerard's time, still had a great trade particularly with Newfoundland, a trade later shared also by the other ports—Lyme, Weymouth and Melcombe Regis. Blandford is described as 'a faire Markett Towne, pleasantlie seated upon the River . . . well inhabitted and of good Traffique'. Shaftesbury was a 'faire Thorough Faire, much frequented by Travellers to and from London', while of Sherborne, near his own residence at Trent, Gerard writes, 'This Towne for Largenesse, Frequencie of Inhabitants, and quicke Marketts, giveth place to none in these Partes.'

Some details of the gentry of Dorset during the seventeenth century may be gained from a Fragment of Autobiography written by Anthony Ashley Cooper, the first earl of Shaftesbury who was born at Wimborne St Giles in 1621. He described how the leading landowners of the eastern part of Dorset met each week at a bowling-green at Handley (Sixpenny Handley), 'Thither resorted Mr. Hastings of Woodland, Sir Gerard Nappier, Mr. Rogers, Sir William Uvedall, Mr. Carent of Woodyats, Mr. Okeden, Mr. Butler, father and son, and Mr. Edward Hooper of Boryds (Boveridge), Mr. Ryves of Raynston, Mr. Holles, Mr. Chafin of Chettle, Mr. Hussey of Edmondsham, Mr. Ernley, Mr. Arney, Sir George Moreton, and myself with several others.' The earl of Shaftesbury's detailed and entertaining sketch of Henry Hastings has often been quoted, and although it neglects the more public-spirited aspects of Hastings' life, it does give an excellent indication of his house and style of life:

> He was low, very strong and very active, of a reddish flaxen hair, his clothes always green cloth, and never all worth when new five pounds. His house was perfectly of the old fashion, in the midst of a large park well-stocked with deer, and near the house rabbits to serve his kitchen, any fish-ponds, and great store of wood and timber; . . . all his neighbours' grounds and royalties were free to him, who bestowed all his time in such sports, but what he borrowed to caress his neighbours' wives and daughters, there being not a woman in all his walks of the degree of a yeoman's wife or under, and under the age of forty, but it was extremely her fault if he were not intimately acquainted with her. This made him very popular, always speaking kindly to the husband, brother or father, who was to boot very welcome to his house whenever he came. There he found beef pudding and small beer in great plenty, a house not so neatly kept as to shame him or his dirty shoes, the great hall strewed with marrow bones, full of hawks perches, hounds, spaniels and terriers, the upper sides of the hall hung with the foxskins of this and the last year's skinning, here and there a polecat intermixed, guns and keepers' and huntsmen's poles in abundance. The parlour was a large long room, as properly furnished; on a great hearth paved with brick lay some terriers and the choicest hounds and spaniels; seldom but two of the great chairs and litters of young cats in them, which were not to be disturbed, he having always three and four attending him at dinner, and a little white round stick of fourteen inches long lying by his trencher, that he might defend such meat as he had no mind to part with to them . . . An oyster-table at the lower end, which was of constant use twice a day all the year round, for he never

Fig 13 Henry Hastings, the seventeenth-century squire of Woodland (This portrait was printed in Hutchins' *History of Dorset* from the original which hung at Wimborne St Giles. It shows Henry Hastings at the age of eighty-seven in 1638; he died in 1650 at the age of ninety-nine)

> failed to eat oysters before dinner and supper through all seasons: the neighbouring town of Poole supplied him with them. He lived to a hundred, never lost his eyesight, but always writ and read without spectacles, and got to horse without help. Until past fourscore he rode to the death of a stag as well as any.

Shaftesbury's autobiography also contains a few details of the gentry of west Dorset, and notes the issue which was soon to divide them so bitterly. He mentions the earl of Bristol and his son, Lord Digby; Sir John Strangways 'very considerable both for estate and family, a wise crafty experienced man . . . a great enemy of the Puritans'; Sir Thomas Trenchard 'a very honest, well-natured, worthy man, a favourer of the Puritans'; Sir John Heal; Mr Coker, 'of a very ancient family, and a most worthy discreet gentleman'; and Mr Gray 'no friend to the Puritan, and by consequence not in love with his neighbours of Dorchester, who were totally devoted that way, being managed by their parson, Mr. White, one of the wisest and subtlest of that sort of men'.

From the early seventeenth century, the sources of information on the life of society increase rapidly, and it is impossible to do more here than mention a few. One aspect of life in which Dorset has been particularly fortunate is in its remarkable number of charities, endowments, almshouses, hospitals and foundations which over the centuries have done an enormous amount to mitigate some of the horrors of poverty and want for countless unfortunates. These charitable endowments range from the very elaborate foundations like the famous almshouse of St John the Baptist and St John the Evangelist which still exists at Sherborne and was founded in 1437 for the support of twelve poor men and four women with a chaplain and a housewife to care for the spiritual and material needs of the inhabitants; to the endowment for occasional doles of money or goods to the needy or for apprenticeing poor children, etc. Many such charities were established during the Middle Ages. There were for example medieval leper hospitals at Allington, Blandford, Lyme Regis, Wimborne, and there were also 'hospitals' or houses providing relief and sustenance for the poor, the sick or the old at Shaftesbury, Wimborne, Wareham, Poole, Dorchester, Bridport and elsewhere, besides the charity provided by the monastic houses. A very large number of charitable endowments were made during the prosperous years of the sixteenth and seventeenth centuries. During the seventeenth century alone, no less than twenty almshouses were founded, of which fifteen are still functioning. Among them the lovely row of almshouses at Wimborne St Giles by the parish church and the entrance to the great house, which were founded by Sir Anthony Ashley in 1624. In addition there were all over the county a host of smaller endowments, like the bequest left by Lady Dorothy Gorges who died in 1649 to provide relief for the poor in the parishes of Gussage, Yetminster and elsewhere. Such charities are still to be found recorded on the 'Bequest boards' in many parish churches. During the eighteenth and nineteenth centuries a very large number of Friendly Societies were formed in the county. There are records of more than 200 of these societies which were founded for mutual help and assistance in times of trouble. Large societies existed at Sherborne, Beaminster, Marnhull, Sturminster Newton and Stalbridge as well as in many smaller villages. One aspect of their activities was the annual feast, often on Whit-Monday, which included a church service and a procession around the town or village in which members carried their banners and staves. These sources of help for the poor were of course in addition to the ordinary relief given by the Overseers of the Poor of each parish and paid for by the Poor Rate.

There were also a surprisingly large number of free schools in Dorset, many of them dating from the sixteenth century or earlier. There was a medieval school at Sherborne, the forerunner of the grammar school, which was refounded there in the reign of Edward VI. At Wimborne also there was probably a medieval school, refounded during the sixteenth century. A grammar school was established in Gillingham during the reign of Henry VIII, and another in Dorchester by Thomas Hardye of Frampton in 1579. These were, and continued to be important and influential schools. But there were also a host of smaller schools, some of them dignified by the title of grammar schools, others aiming to do no more than provide the basic 'reading writing and casting of accounts'. There were small grammar schools at Evershot, Netherbury, Broadwindsor and elsewhere, and free elementary schools in a great many villages, such as the school at Yetminster founded with an endowment left by the eminent scientist Robert Boyle in 1717 where twenty boys could be instructed. The early nineteenth century also saw the establishment of a great many dame schools, evening schools for poor children at several places and a great number of Sunday schools at which elementary education was given as well as more specially religious instruction. Dr Andrew Bell one of the great early nineteenth-century pioneers of education for the poor and a foremost exponent of the system of teaching by monitors was rector of Swanage during the early years of the century. Bell was the power behind the foundation of the immensely influential, and typically named, National Society for the Education of the Poor in the Principles of the Church of England, and the first branch of the society was founded in Dorset in 1812.

The great contrast between the society of Dorset at any time up to the later part of the last century and the society of the twentieth century is how very self-contained and isolated it was. A glance at any of the nineteenth-century directories is enough to show what a great number of different craftsmen and traders were to be found even in the small villages. In the little market towns like Cerne, Wimborne and Beaminster, the variety of crafts and services which could be obtained was even wider, while the larger towns like Poole, Dorchester or Weymouth could provide almost anything that could possibly be required. In the village of Yetminster in 1848 nearly twenty different crafts and trades were carried on including a saddler, several boot and shoe makers, a glazier, maltster, tailor etc. In the little market town of Cranborne at the same time some twenty-five different trades were to be found as well as farmers, innkeepers, carriers etc. Trades at Cranborne included bricklayers, plasterers, a straw-bonnet maker, a plumber and glazier, a cooper, four wheelwrights and two smiths. This self-sufficiency which met all temporal and spiritual wants and provided a secure basis of community life had characterised these little towns and villages since their earliest beginnings.

We get some glimpses of this society from the official records, particularly from those of the Quarter Sessions. We see its concern for good order and public decency in scores of cases like that of Thomas Perriam of Charmouth who was sent to Dorchester gaol for three days in 1625 for keeping 'a common tipling house without licence'. And there were constant disputes between parishes over their responsibilities for maintaining paupers, bastard children, and so on. For example, in 1631 a vagrant woman, Agnes Day, gave birth to a baby girl, Thomasine, in the parish of Long Crichel; a few weeks later she abandoned the baby in a field at Stourpaine, and thereafter disappeared completely, leaving the two parishes to settle the question of which was to be responsible for baby Thomasine. After prolonged controversy it was decided by the justices that the child should be kept by Stourpaine but that Long Crichel should contribute towards her maintenance. The same sort of cases occur again and again, year after year.

But though the society was self-contained and independent, it was certainly not static. By the end of the seventeenth century, great and rapid changes were already very apparent. There was a great growth in population; far-reaching changes were taking place in agriculture; the older industries, particularly the cloth trade, were declining in face of competition from other parts of the country. The problem of paupers and unemployed vagrants became more and more pressing. Increasingly there were appeals to Quarter Sessions as from Cerne and Milton in 1665 that they were overwhelmed with poor people because of decay in trade; or the complaints from all over the county, for example in 1695, about the great member of 'loose and idle persons' who were demanding relief.

During the eighteenth century conditions for a majority of the inhabitants of Dorset worsened very considerably, and by the early nineteenth century the county had already become a byword for the low wages paid to its agricultural labourers, and it retained this reputation throughout the century. When Sir F. M. Eden visited the county in the 1790s to collect material for his great survey of the State of the Poor (published in 1797), he found a shocking state of affairs. At Blandford he found that farm labourers' wages were 6s or 7s per week. There were thirty-six inmates in the workhouse and more than a hundred others receiving regular parish relief. Eden commented that 'The rapid rise of the Poor's Rate in this parish is generally attributed to the high price of provisions, the smallness of wages, and the consolidation of small farms, and the consequent depopulation of villages, which obliges small farmers to turn labourers or servants . . . It is said that there are now only two farms in Durweston . . . which contained about 30 small farms 20 years ago. And what is more singular the town of Abbey Milton, which was formerly the central market of the county, is now a fish pond . . .'

With the ending of the Napoleonic Wars in 1815 and the consequent recession in agriculture, conditions for the labourers got even worse. Population was rising rapidly and by 1815 already 13 per cent of the total population of Dorset was in receipt of poor relief, and the number forced to apply for help from the parish grew steadily during the next few years. It was a time of unparalleled poverty, degradation and misery in the county. By 1830, the appallingly low wages, bad conditions and incredibly long hours of work stirred even the normally passive Dorset labourers to protest, and many joined in the widespread rioting, rick-burning and machine breaking which swept through southern England during the autumn of that year—the notorious 'Captain Swing' riots. There were two main areas of rioting in Dorset, the central chalklands between Dorchester and Wimborne, and the traditionally lawless and unruly region of Cranborne Chase and the area between Cranborne and Stalbridge. Both these areas were characterised by very large estates and vast farms. It is noticeable that the smaller farms in the dairying, pastoral area of west Dorset were not affected. In November 1830, with news coming in of risings and riots in neighbouring counties, labourers around Bere Regis began assembling to demand a 10s weekly wage, instead of the 6s or 7s a week on which they were expected to live. The movement spread rapidly to the areas of Wareham and Puddletown, where ricks were burned and threshing machines broken. More serious rioting followed around Blandford and Shaftesbury, involving very large numbers of labourers. At Sixpenny Handley, for example, on 23 November 1830, a magistrate reported that 'had we committed for participating in and aiding the burning of machinery, we might have committed two thirds of the labouring population of the district'. Threatening letters were received by a number of landowners. One to Mr Castleman, whose estates were in the Wimborne area, declared 'Sunday night your house shall come down to the Ground for you are an inhuman monster and we will dash out your brains—Banks and your sett aught to be sent to Hell. The Hanley Torches have not forgot you.' In all there were more than forty separate riots and disturbances in the county.

Meanwhile, there was frenzied activity by the county magistrates. Great numbers of special constables were sworn in, the yeomanry and the coastguards were brought in to help quell the mobs, and vigorous arrangements were made by landowners to defend their property. Some concessions were made. Farmers in the Puddletown area agreed to raise wages to 10s a week; in the Gillingham area wages were increased to 9s. At the same time large numbers of men were arrested for taking part in unlawful assemblies and were imprisoned. Not all were captured of course. During a rising at Winfrith, James Frampton of Moreton, one of the most active and unpopular of the magistrates, grabbed one man from the mob, but the man slipped out of his smock and escaped leaving his smock behind. By early December more troops arrived, and the riots died out.

In January 1831, sixty-two prisoners were tried by a Special Commission at Dorchester, of whom thirteen were sentenced to transportation for life for their part in the attempt to gain a living wage. A petition was presented to the king to get these sentences reduced, but as Mary Frampton, sister of James Frampton, wrote in her journal, 'Fortunately . . . as they were already on board the transports and the wind fair, the petition would be too late. Care was taken at the deportation of these men . . . to send them to those parts of New Zealand and New Holland where their agricultural knowledge and labour might be useful. Thus very probably at a future time rendering our disturbances here a blessing to our Antipodes.' The few temporary improvements in wages secured in 1830 were quickly lost and the Dorset farm workers were soon in as desperate a condition as before. This gave rise to the famous attempt to found the Friendly Society of Agricultural Labourers at Tolpuddle in 1833. Some forty labourers joined this society and it was hoped that the society would be the forerunner of others in Dorset. But the labourers reckoned without the determination of the government and the local magistrates, with memories of the 'Captain Swing riots' of 1830 still fresh. In particular they had to contend with the magistrate chiefly concerned with the Tolpuddle area, James Frampton, passionately concerned with maintaining law and order and with stamping out anything that might lead to civil disobedience and unrest.

The story of the Tolpuddle Martyrs, their trial, transportation and the subsequent outcry aroused has been too frequently and fully told to require retelling here, but the smashing of the embryonic union at Tolpuddle in 1834 meant that the Dorset labourer had no hope or method of improving his wages and conditions. The evidence of numerous observers, parliamentary reports and royal commissions bears witness to the wretched and miserable lot of the labourers, working long hours in appalling conditions and living in grossly overcrowded inadequate cottages. The Report on the Employment of Women and Children in Agriculture published in 1843 contains horrifying accounts of conditions in Dorset, and shows that female labour was common in the fields and that children were also employed from the age of six or seven. A further Report on the subject in 1867 shows that conditions remained as bad. At Holwell 'they cannot keep any boys in the school after 7; they go out as carter boys'; at Marnhull 'a good many go at 6 and 7'. The Parliamentary Commissioner reported that 'the proportion of boy labour regularly employed upon farms is larger than in any county visited by me . . .' He also observed that the cottages were very bad, 'The estate of Lord Rivers . . . is notorious for its bad cottages. And such villages as Bere Regis, Fordington, Winfrith, Cranborne or Charminster (in which there is an average of seven persons to a house) . . . are a disgrace to the owners of the land and contain many cottages unfit for human habitation.' In the Cerne and Wimborne districts he found that 16 per cent of the cottages had one bedroom only, and all over the county there was an absence of 'the most obvious sanitary precautions'. At Corfe Castle, the incumbent, the Rev E. S. Bankes, reported that the cottages were very bad: 'I have one family of eight living in an outhouse built for a calf, and one cottage on the heath (divided into three) contained 33 souls at the last census.' The only redeeming feature of the county was the large gardens generally allotted to labourers. But for them the commissioner thought that 'the wages would sometimes hardly be sufficient to support life'.

The Report also noted that in some districts, particularly the Blackmoor Vale and Blandford areas, many labourers' families supplemented the family income by the manufacture of gloves, but commented that it was 'very unremunerative work, and can only be made to pay by long hours of very hard work'. Another feature of rural life reported on was the village schools. These faced great difficulties because of the demand for child labour, and because of the opposition of the farmers. The farmers felt that if children were educated they would not stay in the villages, but would seek a better life elsewhere. That this fear was justified is shown by Durweston village school in 1867, where, out of 187 children educated there, 153 had left the parish.

In considering the society of Dorset during the nineteenth century, it is difficult to achieve a correct balance and perspective. The miserable conditions of many farm labourers existed side by side with a great deal of wealth and affluence, particularly in the mid-nineteenth century which was a period of prosperity for Dorset farming. It is clear from the pages of Hardy, or from the poems of William Barnes, that not all labourers were affected by the grinding poverty which so many observers saw in the county. The great number of solid nineteenth-century houses and shops to be found in Weymouth, Bridport, Poole, Swanage, Dorchester, Gillingham, and in nearly all other towns and villages, show that here was another section of society which was enjoying a reasonable prosperity. In the great houses at the centre of each of the vast estates which so dominated the county, and in the solid stone farmhouses, the poor could see a life of comparative ease and luxury, very far removed from their own existence. An indoor staff of twenty-seven was kept by Lord Shaftesbury at Wimborne St Giles, and the Drax family in the great house at Charborough with its extensive park and seemingly endless park walls, like the Digbys, Pitt-Rivers, Fox-Strangways, Welds, Sturts, Bankes and many other families, lived in similar style on their respective estates. Perhaps the best illustration of the affluence and self-assurance of the nineteenth-century landowners is to be found in the great mass of Bryanston House built for Lord Portman during the 1890s, its stark uncompromising outline, emphasised by the bright red of its brickwork, set on a hill-top, dominating the town of Blandford.

By the 1870s, however, agriculture was entering upon a long period of depression, and the drift away from the villages and into the towns becomes very marked. Earlier, although some hardy souls had achieved it, it had been an immensely difficult undertaking for a labourer to get out of the county without capital and with no convenient transport. Some improvement in wages towards the end of the century, coinciding with the coming of the railways, enabled more and more labourers to go to the expanding industrial towns of the Midlands and North, or even to emigrate overseas, this leading to the depopulation of so many Dorset villages which was discussed in Chapter 3. This great decline in the population of the villages is masked in the overall figures for the population of the county by the vast increases in the population of a few centres such as Poole and Portland.

SELECT BIBLIOGRAPHY

E. Cockburn	*The Almshouses of Dorset* (1970)
J. P. Ferris	'The Gentry of Dorset on the Eve of the Civil War' (*Genealogist Magazine*, vol 15, no 3, 1965)
E. J. Hobsbawm and G. Rudé	*Captain Swing* (1969)
J. Marlow	*The Tolpuddle Martyrs* (1971)
A. Oswald	*The County Houses of Dorset* (1959)
E. H. Roscoe (ed)	*The Marn'll Book* (1952)

Chapter 9 THE IMPACT OF THE TWENTIETH CENTURY

DORSET in the twentieth century has seen tremendous changes and great acceleration of developments which were already taking place during the previous century. The first and most obvious of these developments has been the continuing increase in population. The 1801 Census recorded 114,452 persons living in the county. By 1851 the figure had risen to 184,380, and by 1901 it had reached 202,984. In 1971 the figure was 361,919. This continuing population increase has inevitably led to enormous expansion in some towns and villages, and to the creation for the first time in the county of a really large urban area in the gigantic growth of Poole and its hinterland. Poole and Bournemouth together now form the largest non-industrial conurbation in the British Isles. Weymouth, too, with a population in 1971 of 42,349, is a prosperous and expanding town. Other towns have also grown rapidly, notably Dorchester and Swanage, and growth has dramatically affected other places such as Wimborne and Sherborne where twentieth-century housing developments can be seen radiating out from the medieval centres, particularly on the northern and eastern sides. Population growth has been very uneven in the county, and the dramatic increase in the population of some few urban centres and villages, has been accompanied by a continuing decline or at any rate lack of growth in many villages and some smaller towns. Local government reorganisation in 1973–4 has enlarged the county boundaries of Dorset and added greatly to its population. The new Dorset consists of the whole of the ancient county together with Bournemouth, Christchurch, the

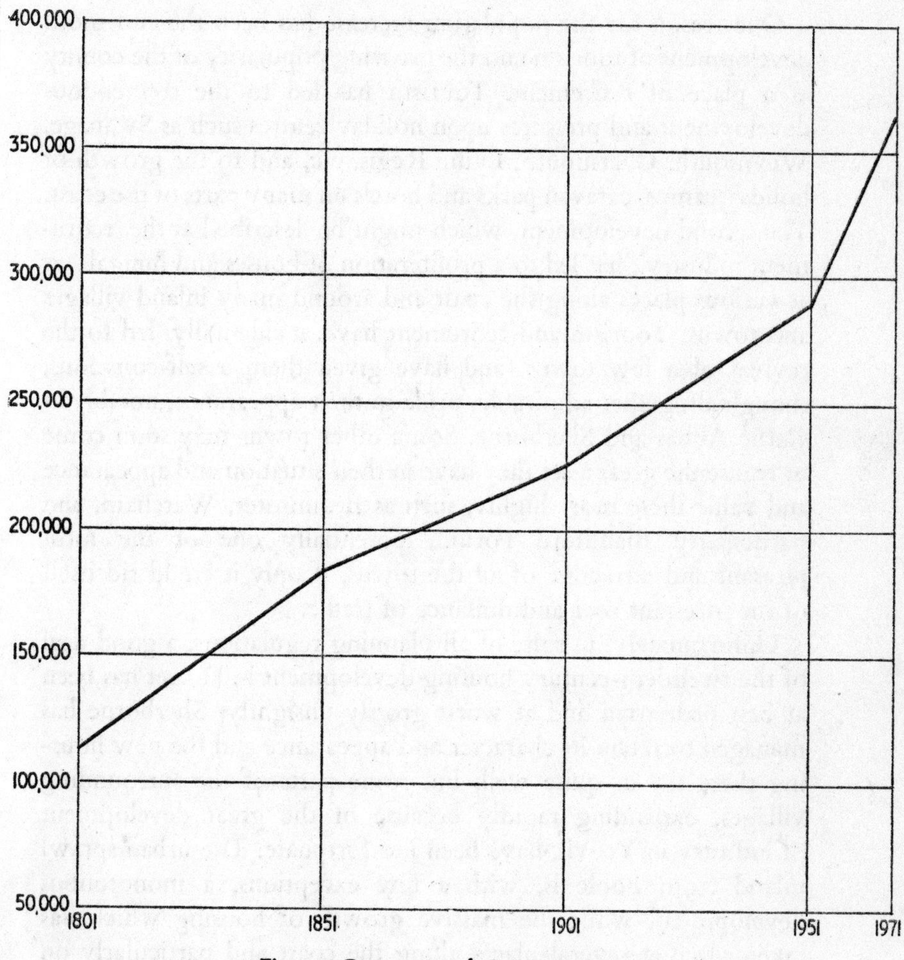

Fig 14 County population 1801–1971

parishes of St Leonards and St Ives, Hurn, part of the parishes of Sopley and Christchurch East. The population of the new county is 553,000.

One reason for the population increase has been the enormous development of tourism and the growing popularity of the county as a place of retirement. Tourism has led to the tremendous development and pressures upon holiday centres such as Swanage, Weymouth, Charmouth, Lyme Regis, etc, and to the growth of holiday camps, caravan parks and hotels on many parts of the coast. The second development, which might be described as the 'retirement industry', has led to a proliferation of houses and bungalows at various places along the coast and around many inland villages and towns. Tourism and retirement have, incidentally, led to the revival of a few towns, and have given them a self-conscious, though altogether admirable, pride in their appearance, notably at Cerne Abbas and Sherborne. Some other towns may soon come to realise the great asset they have in their situation and appearance and value these more highly, such as Beaminster, Wareham, and particularly Blandford Forum, potentially one of the most pleasant and attractive of all the towns, if only it could rid itself of the incessant roar and nuisance of traffic.

Unfortunately, in spite of all planning regulations, a good deal of the twentieth-century housing development in Dorset has been at best pedestrian and at worst grossly unsightly. Sherborne has managed to retain its character and appearance and the new housing there fits in quite well, but some parts of the surrounding villages, expanding rapidly because of the great development of industry in Yeovil, have been less fortunate. The urban sprawl inland from Poole is, with a few exceptions, a monotonous development, while the massive growth of housing which has taken place at several places along the coast and particularly on the Island of Portland and around Portland harbour, on the most dramatic and powerful piece of coastal scenery in southern England, is a standing reproach to the twentieth century. In contrast, a few modern buildings do show what can be achieved by careful planning and design, and by the use of suitable materials;

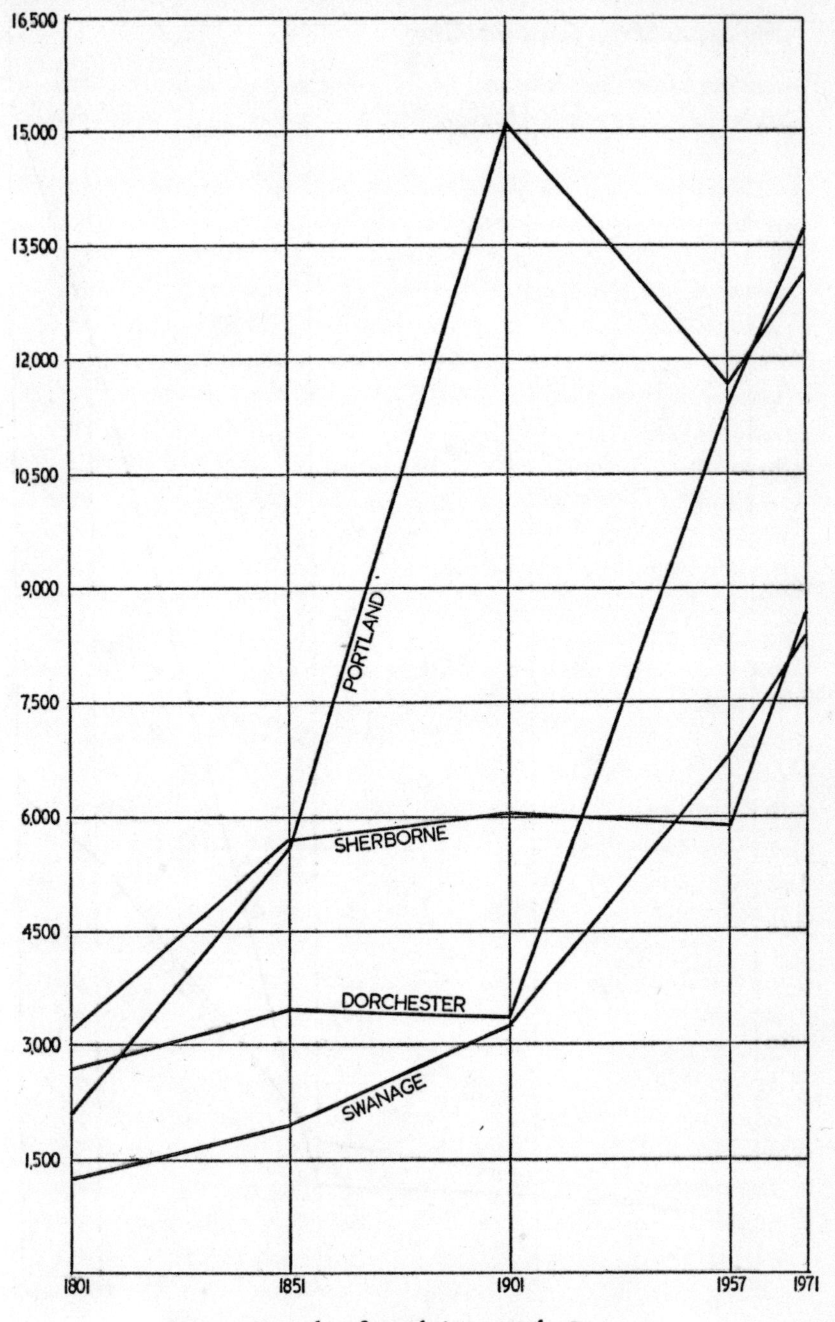

Fig 15 Examples of population growth 1801–1971

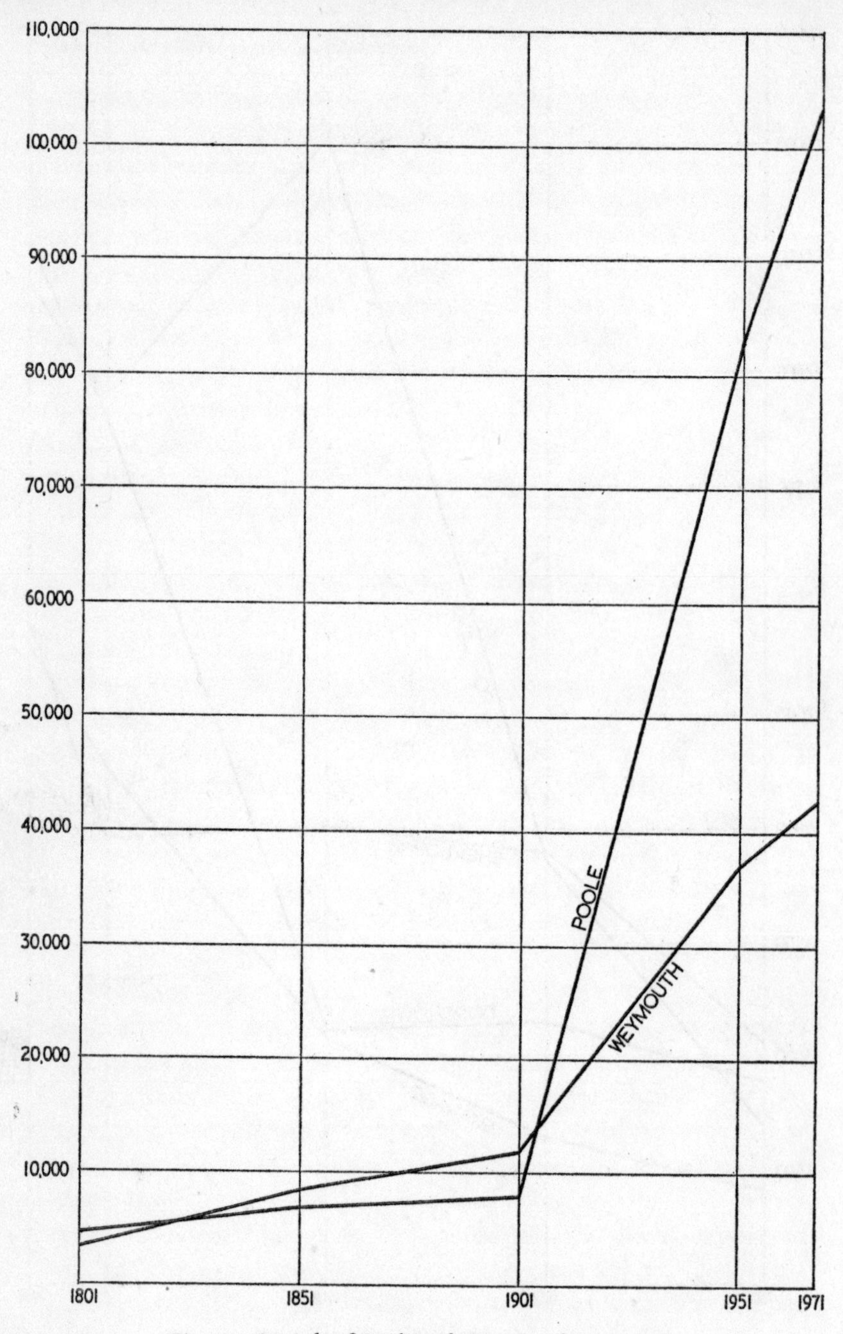

Fig 16 Growth of Poole and Weymouth 1801–1971

the libraries and schools built by the County Council during the past few years are particularly good examples of this.

There have also been great changes in agriculture, which, since 1939, has developed in ways quite different from the old traditional pattern of Dorset farming. Sheep have declined greatly in importance, and have virtually disappeared from many areas, and the old mixed farming of which sheep formed such an important element, has been replaced by vast cereal crops, particularly on the chalk downlands. This in turn has led to the ploughing up of a great deal of downland and to the consequent destruction of many archaeological remains of great importance and significance in the history of the county, and to the rooting out of many hedgerows with a quite dramatic effect on the appearance of the landscape.

Since 1939 the land held by the military services and by various government departments has increased enormously, in spite of all the pledges given at the time that areas commandeered for military purposes during the war would be handed back when the war ended. Military occupation is at its most blatant and arrogant in the Isle of Purbeck, and in particular at Tyneham, though the army is likely to be forced soon to relinquish at least part of this area. In addition, the Atomic Energy Establishment at Winfrith, a principal centre for reactor systems research, occupies about 1,100 acres of heathland, though its large complex of buildings certainly fits into the landscape well, much better than the eyesore at nearby Bovington or some of the other army camps, and the Admiralty developments at Portland.

In thinking about developments in Dorset during the twentieth century, it is easy to become despondent. A great deal of damage and destruction has been wrought on the historic landscape and on many towns and villages, much of it needlessly destructive or thoughtlessly planned. In many towns and villages life is made hideous by the continuous thunder of heavy through-traffic, as in Dorchester, Bridport, Wimborne and elsewhere. Many places along the coast are ruined by unsightly developments or are threatened by the mass of tourists who visit them and the consequent traffic, litter and congestion they bring.

At the same time, however, there remain in the county probably more areas of great charm and beauty, and more places where historic continuity and development can be observed, than in any other area of comparable size in England. Few counties can match the views to be obtained from the chalk downlands and high ground all over the county, none can compete with the number and importance of standing archaeological remains. The profusion of excellent and supremely attractive historic manor houses, farmhouses and cottages to be found throughout the county is still a constant source of delight to the traveller. While villages such as Ashmore, Hinton St Mary, Cerne Abbas, Charminster, Beaminster and a host of others throughout the county, and towns like Wareham, Sturminster Newton, Sherborne or Lyme Regis retain an immense charm and still give to the visitor a remarkably powerful sense of their historic continuity.

Note: The author is grateful to his colleague, David Wilde, for his help with Figures 14, 15 and 16.

GENERAL BIBLIOGRAPHY

A. R. Bayley, *The Civil War in Dorset* (1910)
J. H. Bettey, *The Island and Royal Manor of Portland* (1970)
J. Brocklebank, *Affpuddle* (1968)
A. L. Clegg, *The History of Wimborne Minster* (1960)
R. Douch, *Handbook of Local History—Dorset* (1962)
A. Fägersten, *The Place Names of Dorset* (1933)
N. H. Field and J. Bugler, *The Guide to the Field Monuments of Dorset* (1973)
J. Fowler, *Medieval Sherborne* (1951)
R. Good, *The Old Roads of Dorset* (1966)
J. Hutchins, *The History and Antiquities of Dorset*, 3rd ed (1861–70)
B. Kerr, *Bound to the Soil* (1968)
R. Legg, *Purbeck* (1972)
R. Lloyd, *Dorset Elizabethans* (1967)
J. H. Lucking, *Railways of Dorset* (1968)
John Newman and Nikolaus Pevsner, *The Buildings of England—Dorset* (1972)
A. Oswald, *Country Houses of Dorset* (1959)
Royal Commission on Historical Monuments (England), *Dorset* (1952–)
A. Sandison, *Trent in Dorset* (1969)
H. P. Smith, *The History of the Borough and County of Poole* (1951)
L. Sydenham, *Shaftesbury and Its Abbey* (1959)
C. Taylor, *The Making of the English Landscape—Dorset* (1970)
Victoria County History, *Dorset*, vol II (1908), vol III (1968)
M. B. Weinstock, *Old Dorset* (1967)

INDEX